The Darkness & the Light

Angel Power

authorHOUSE

AuthorHouse™
1663 Liberty Drive
Bloomington, IN 47403
www.authorhouse.com
Phone: 1 (800) 839-8640

© *2016 Angel Power. All rights reserved.*

No part of this book may be reproduced, stored in a retrieval system, or transmitted by any means without the written permission of the author.

Published by AuthorHouse 10/06/2016

ISBN: 978-1-5246-2248-0 (sc)
ISBN: 978-1-5246-2247-3 (e)

Library of Congress Control Number: 2016912471

Print information available on the last page.

Any people depicted in stock imagery provided by Thinkstock are models, and such images are being used for illustrative purposes only. Certain stock imagery © Thinkstock.

This book is printed on acid-free paper.

Because of the dynamic nature of the Internet, any web addresses or links contained in this book may have changed since publication and may no longer be valid. The views expressed in this work are solely those of the author and do not necessarily reflect the views of the publisher, and the publisher hereby disclaims any responsibility for them.

In Memory of the Forgotten.

Born for the Unborn.

Thank You

To my family:

My mom and brother who always supported me,
And who stood by me throughout the darkness, providing some light.
I regret all the stress I caused you and I'll do everything I can to make it right.
To earth angels who just happened to be in the right place
And the lady from the church who helped me without even meeting me or seeing my face.
To my childhood counsellor who I met when I was hospitalized at fourteen, who encouraged me and listened to my poetry.
To those rare individuals and few community agencies who supported me and showed me compassion in the past,
To those who encouraged me to write and supported my work; the sense of empowerment you gave me will always last.
To my Higher Power, my Spirit Guide, my Angels, for blessings and second chances and strength.
These are just some of who I wish to thank.
From the few friends who have supported me at times throughout the journey,
To the kind Christian neighbours who used to live across the street; to pets who were always there for me, and the few good friends of my mom;
When I count all those I'm grateful for the list gets rather long.
Thank you each and thank you all,
From the bottom of my heart and deep within my soul.

Author's Note

This book is a collection of poetry I've written over many years of my life; through the dark times and the light. It is therefore in two parts; the good and the bad. Although most of it does, *some* of the poetry I've written does not necessarily reflect how I feel today. It is how I felt in the moments of darkness. If when reading through the darkness you feel disturbed, overwhelmed, angry, saddened or discouraged, then please consider what it was like to live it. Just like I had to, I urge the reader to keep going. Have hope and faith that there will be a happy ending.

Disclaimer

This is a work of creative nonfiction written from my personal perspective.

It is deeply personal so I do not pretend to be objective.

However, where it was necessary, to protect myself and the privacy of other's, I changed or omitted names,

But as Shakespeare taught, what's in a name? Even without it the truth remains the same.

Part 1

The Darkness

X Rated Truth & Political Poetry for a Patriarchal Society

Introduction

I am a person; a woman, a daughter, a sister.

I've been a delinquent, a run-away, an addict, a stripper.

I've been in relationships that were severely violent and abusive.

I've been preyed on and conned but I did not choose this.

I was once a child.

As a child I was lured and misled, so as a teen was it a surprise I went wild?

I've been places I wish I'd never been and I've seen things I wish I'd never seen.

As a youth I was trapped in toxic relationships and failed by the system.

When I sought help I faced additional hardships, so I had to rely on my own insight and wisdom.

Courtroom corruption, the entire production I've witnessed.

I'm held accountable for every single thing I do but corrupt cops can terrorize me and get away with it- just a few more on my fantasy hit list.

They sicken me, the one who gets away with sick evil deeds and cruel violence; He who buys silence.

I have disgust for the corrupt criminal justice system in which I grew up in, in which we teach children truth and trust is written.

But I grew up fast and that didn't last and now I have a very different description.

I'll expose the corrupt criminal lawyer

Paid to advocate for a child destroyer.

I'll expose all the corruption and injustices I see.

I cannot look the other way or sit quietly.

I've been dehumanized, degraded and have gone unheard,

But I'm unbreakable; a survivor and I'm about to ruffle some feathers now through the power of the written word.

Some may find my writing shocking, offensive or disturbing

But each raw word is real.

These are the feelings we sometimes feel.

It's necessary to vent in order to heal.

So, in a world where a child can basically see soft porn on a billboard or watching daytime TV,

Please don't be offended by me.

We live in a society obsessed with sexuality, money and greed,

I just write accordingly.

I write based on what I've felt and what I've seen.

Chapter 1

Domestic Violence, Victim Blaming & Secondary Victimization

Empty Shell

They took my eyes
When they changed the way I see.
They took my voice
When they refused to hear me.

They took my innocence
When I was exploited, corrupted, and violated.
They took my passion
When they made me feel weak and jaded.

They took my freedom
When they made me fear the world.
They robbed me of my womanhood
When I was just a girl.

I am now an empty shell.
My life has become a living hell.
I was damaged so badly I don't know if I'll ever be well.
I was once full of life and had so much to give
But I was robbed of all I had and now I'm utterly discouraged.

They robbed me of my spirit
When they drained me of all my energy.
They diminished all trust I had
When friends and family members turned on me.

They stripped me of my trust in my intuitive soul
When they made me doubt myself.

They made me look like a fool
When I put my trust in someone else.

They took my identity
When they made me dislike the real me.
They took my mind
When they changed how I think.

The real me is now suppressed.
Soon there will be no sign of my true self left.
I've become someone else to adapt and survive
But someday when it's safe, my soul will be revived.
Until that day, I continue to hide.

Bitter Sweet

I miss what we once had,

But I can't look at you the same because you hurt me so bad.

I looked at you with admiration. I thought you were a divine creation.

I've seen love in your eyes and I've seen Satan.

You were once my hero and I believed you rescued me and would keep me safe.

But you turned on me. There's no love in your eyes, I just see hate.

You gave me hope; I thought I had a reason to excel.

I changed my whole life because you promised me help.

But now I'm alone and it seems even without anyone, I'm still capable of doing well.

I always tell myself, next time I'll leave at the first sign of abuse,

But by that time it's too late, I already love you.

Finger Prints on My Thighs

Finger prints on my thighs,
Tears in my eyes,
The pillow silences my cries,
His apologies are lies.

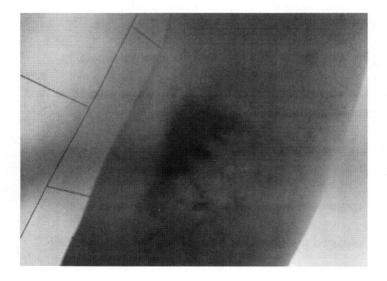

Abuse Awareness

Abuse is misuse produced from youth.
Abuse is the way he spoke to me, touched me.
Abuse is perhaps the only love I've ever seen.
Abuse is when he yells, "Put your face down and your ass up, bitch!" and you know you must obey.
Abuse is when you feel like a slave.
Abuse occurs each day in several different ways.

Financial abuse is when he takes your money and you have no access.
Environmental abuse is when he locks you in, throws things, and your beautiful home becomes a war zone and a vandalized mess.
Sexual abuse- its torture being held down on that bed.
Emotional abuse is mind games that get to your head.
Physical abuse- you never forget that first push, punch, or slap.
Social abuse is when he humiliates you in public, makes a scene, and you freeze, you feel trapped.
Verbal abuse is when he calls you names.
A victim can't help but feel ashamed.

When it comes to abuse, we need stricter penalties and laws.
It's one of the system's biggest flaws.
Search deep for the cause.
Find out what provokes the violence and why society's reaction is silence,

Because when a young girl is misused to this extent and when she's taught math and French but had no idea what abuse meant until she lies battered and beaten on the cement, When is her justice sent?

You can temporarily put a man behind bars but abuse is with her for life- she'll always have the scars.
And within months he's back on the street and a new innocent woman is battered and beat.
It's like the feeling of defeat.
Finding the courage to take a stand and charge this man, like a footstep in the sand,
It's so quickly covered up.

Then people ask, "Why do abused women stay?"
Each night they pray, "Please let things be different today."
Empathize. Don't criticize.
Sympathize.
See the black eyes, and hear the cries.

With society's support we can conquer abuse.
We have shelters and support groups
But this is all to help her after the fact, after the broken heart and after the stinging slap.

It's what leads to it before that we ignore.
So then, what's the use?
Help *prevent* abuse.

Life Altering Moments

Whack! Whack! Goes my head into the dash
Because of the self-control you lack.
My vision goes blurry until I see black.
I still feel the pain in my back because of your last attack.

You never stopped until the neighbour came and said he'd called the cops. You would have kept beating me but that made you take off.
I'm telling the cops I'm fine as I bleed from the scalp
And I saw your boy watch but he didn't even help.
This time bruises, next time welts.
You'll never know how I felt
Lying there.
Booze from your breath is all I smelled.
I hoped maybe
By some miracle I didn't lose our baby.

Lost in the Darkness

You see a girl walking down the street.
In her eyes if you look deep you can see she's discouraged and weak.
She lost everything including the baby she planned to keep.
You see a vulnerable girl but she's becoming a woman who defies defeat.

That morning you saw an innocent girl and realized your mistake,
But by my second decade, I've been beaten and burned and raped.
Didn't that take my innocence away?
Loving was always a mistake.
Isn't it something I should hate?
That all changed so quickly and it was too late.

I loved before and initially that love was great.
I was so sure it was real I couldn't believe it was fake.
I was so sure it was right but it was a mistake.
If I've only been loved by men who are full of hate,
Did love ever exist in the first place?

People look at me and have no idea what's going on in my head.
They assume things are fine but they don't know I'm almost dead.
They don't feel my grief.
"You've got your whole life ahead of you", the stranger said.
Alone at night when no one sees, I cry myself to sleep in an unfamiliar bed.

Once upon a Time

Once upon a time I was going to be just fine,
Before they exploited my body and corrupted my mind.
I once could see but now I'm blind.
I once had hope which now I fail to find.

All childhood sins were made with innocent intentions
But each mistake altered my fate, I just wasn't paying attention.
An obsession of avoiding rejection has led to my regression.
A valuable lesson: They'll destroy you if they get the chance. Don't let them.

Once upon a time I thought I could be anything I dreamed of.
Long before I knew of barriers and thought I had equality and freedom.
A happy ending I believed in, before I understood the king's kingdom.
I was a lost girl in a man's world full of predators, evil and demons.

Once upon a time I thought judicial justice existed. Now I just have faith in karmic retribution.
A long time ago I may have turned to others for help. Now I chose seclusion.
Others may misguide me;
I turn inward for a solution.

There is no knight in shining armour.
So, the princess or damsel in distress has no choice left but to dust off her dress,
Look at the situation and reassess and keep going while trying her best
Cherishing anything she has left, gradually making progress.
Because fairy-tales are fiction and there is no easy happily ever after like the prediction.
"I'll save you!"
Say it to yourself with conviction.

My story was written by some factors that influence my fate
But I determine how the story ends based on the choices I make.
How much can my character take?
As in most stories, the villain can never make the good guy break.

Lifeless

His face,
It taunts me.
This place,
It haunts me.
The reality of my life makes me nauseous.
The sweet spell of my knife is toxic.
I'll stop cutting when I have a reason to stop it.
I spare others and take the rage out on myself and the anger is constant.
The alternative is more dangerous though, and believe me you don't want it.

I never called the police and when they were called I refused to say a thing but they tricked me.
They said they already knew everything and they convinced me I could save another girl from experiencing the same thing.
Yet during my pursuit for justice there was a slight interruption - courtroom corruption.
Tell me that sixteen violent charges like sexual assault, forcible confinement, assault with a weapon, assault causing bodily harm, and more were not dismissed,
And then when I can't take it anymore, they arrest *me* for driving my car off a cliff.
Tell me there's something I missed!

He got away with it all and he abused me on every level.
What's the victim to do but fantasize about a gun and shovel?

They told me if I didn't leave I'd end up dead
But when I tried to leave, I was re-victimized instead.

If he ever comes after me again, I'll reach for a gun before I ever reach for a phone to call 911.
The message that's been sent is I'm worthless; he's untouchable, you can't trust the police and reporting abuse causes more harm than good.
They laughed at me and laugh they should.
He didn't take abusing me seriously and he shouldn't.
He didn't think anyone would make him pay and they wouldn't.
He didn't think I could do anything about it and I couldn't.
Fear has become no more than a neutral state. You have to value your life to fear death
And I HAVE NOTHING LEFT.

When you know that at any moment he could come back and your life could be endangered, life becomes worse than death.
I'm becoming less afraid of them and more afraid of myself.
I fear if I'm attacked again what I might do to someone else.
He can't hurt me anymore. I've already endured the worst pain I could have imagined.
Because ever since the beginning of all that has happened, I've become immune to pain and calm in chaos and crisis.
I don't want to be like this.
You can try to kill me,
But ever since he destroyed the life that grew inside me
I am already lifeless.

Chapter 2
Inequality

Untitled

If it's a small world after all, then why am I so lonely?
If love is a necessity, I guess pain is too.
That's what love is isn't it? The pain that comes from attachment is the greatest pain I ever knew.
If you get what you give, why do I have nothing but a broken heart?
If it's a fair game then why wasn't I given a fair start?

Sugar & Spice and Everything Nice

They never told me my worth would be determined by my sexuality.
They never told me I'd still be trapped even when freed.
They never told me I'd be deprived of equality.
They never told me it was a sex, greed, deceit driven society.
They never told me,
But I quickly began to see.

They never told me I'd always have to live in fear.
They never told me the odds were against me.
They never told me I'd never be taken seriously.
They never told me they doubted I'd succeed.
They never prepared me for what I had to take
And I made mistake after mistake.

They said, "…Sugar and spice and everything nice,"
But they didn't prepare me for the never ending fight
And I've been beat up and beat down my whole life.

My people weren't even considered people until relatively recently,
Yet we seem to forget what women went through easily.
Perhaps it's because we women react passively naturally.

I was just a girl in a man's world.
A defiant princess in a patriarchal society,
They should have told me.

Those who are Struggle (and Those who Don't)

I am the struggling black man.
I'm juggling defending against relentless stereotypes, ignorance and nonsense,
Doing the best I can, behind before I began.
My ancestors were punished for having skin darker tanned.
We've faced deprivation of rights and land.
Today, I still have to fight with twice the might just to stand in the same position as someone whose skin is white.
Through these eyes, the world isn't quite right.
So my people have pushed for change
And we are still fighting today.

I am the mistreated child about to go wild after being corrupted by the world.
I am the beaten boy, the degraded girl.
I am in a powerless position and I fend for myself.
I survive by my own innate strength.
I had no one else and there was no one who would help.
I was misled by following adult's rule,
Through my young eyes the world is cruel.

I am an aboriginal
Many of my people are displaced, murdered or missing, on the streets or in the penitentiaries.
Has this become our place in the world?
In the land of the free, we are the forgotten people.

Stripped of our identities, robbed of our culture and our land, children stolen from parents, is it surprising where we stand?
More of a set up than a surprise – the white man lied and the government doesn't want to give us any more retribution.
Left oppressed, they let us drink ourselves into their institutions.
They put the drink in my ancestors hand way back when he didn't understand the consequences of what it meant.
I'm now genetically vulnerable and I drink today to drink the pain away of being an unwanted and violated race.

I am a woman.
A Hungarian, an Asian, a Russian, African, or Indian, American or Canadian;
Any woman in the world sacrifices due to her sexuality
I'm the unwillingly married, the murdered and buried, the victim of human trafficking.
I am the one who was forced into female genital mutilation, the one seen as inferior in my nation, the underestimated, underappreciated creator of procreation.
Afraid to walk alone at night, punished for being a woman.
My world is unjust and through my eyes, nothing is right.

I am the abandoned pet, freezing cold on the winter street or dehydrated in the summer's heat.
Puddles are where I drink, wherever and whenever I can I eat.
Every day, I repeat without relief and without peace.
Through my scared eyes, the world is an unfriendly place

I wish I wasn't here and I walk my entire short life trying to escape.
But there is no retreat for my wounded, weak, tired feet.

I am nature - plants, trees, flowers, birds and bees.
I am naturally beautiful, beautifully natural and unique.
As trees, I provide the world with oxygen, as flowers I provide bees their pollen.
But countless ecosystems and habitats are stolen
Forests are destroyed and animals go extinct
Crashing down come the trees and in their place, more stores we don't need.
Nature is destroyed.
Nature – helpless, living beings.

I am the one from an underdeveloped country, the one you hear about on the news.
There is no school to attend, there is no food, and there are limited choices to choose.
Everything is scarce except for my ample obligations and mouths to feed in our overcrowded population.
Dreams seem so far out of reach.
I listen to what the wise villagers preach
But it seems this is where I'll always be – I'll never prosper from here.
Through my eyes, all I've seen are death, famine and disease.
I yearn to be free, to succeed and to be able to live comfortably.

I am the "old money", rich white man
I was born privileged because of my gender, class, and skin.
My whole life I've possessed power and have been told I'd win.

I stand proud.
Shoulders back, chin up, chest out; I'm confident.
I feel entitled to getting what I want because this is how it's always been.
Through my eyes I see countless opportunities.
When I look at the world around me I'm satisfied.
I wouldn't change a thing.

The Punishment Given for Being Women

If she's too heavy she's criticized.
If she shows skin, if she's toned and thin, she's objectified.
When she dresses up and struts her stuff they say she looks like a slut.
Then in a t-shirt and sweats, they say she's a mess and will never find love if she's not looking her best.
She can't win.
It's the punishment of being a woman.

It's a free country but be careful where you go.
Be careful how you dress, talk, look, act and who you get to know.
Like a child, be afraid after dark
And don't walk alone in the park.
Even in the land of the free
We don't have equality.
Prepare to be underpaid.
Prepare for a character assassination if raped,
And prepare for trauma and heartache.

It's a punishment given for being women.
In a patriarchal society, women suffer silently.

In this prison of mine everyone is cold and desensitized.
You'll find evil in their eyes.
Everyone lived sinful lives.
We sold our souls to the devil and we believe his lies.

We're lost in denial and we don't realize.
All we have left are our unanswered outcries, in this prison of mine.

I always have to be on guard and I can't trust anyone.
I have to act hard, always serious, there's no time for fun.
In this prison of mine I'm oppressed and isolated, becoming deeply depressed and jaded.
In this prison of mine
I scream but no one answers my call.
I wish it were a dream
But it's just me and these thick, solid cement walls.

I'm disconnected from the real world.
Every day I'm disrespected and treated like an animal.

This world is my prison
And the inmates are its women.

Chapter 3
The Teen

False Confidence

She floats through the room in her stylish clothes.
Her long hair flows, bouncing as she walks.
They say they're mesmerized by her soulful eyes and act intrigued as she talks.
What she says is deep and profound.
Yet when she speaks no one pays attention, and unless she lets them use her no one is around.

There are guys who want to be with her and there are girls who want to be her.
After seeing the character she portrays they all assume she must be a certain way.
They think she must have it so good
But no one really knows her and she leaves alone thinking, if I could just end it I would.

Most male friends turned on her in the end,
And then, there were the women:
Unjustified jealousy, juvenile, superficial and catty,
And relationships with men were ruined by their insecurities.
They say she's beautiful,
A matter of opinion, she thinks.
Perhaps to some she appears beautiful on the outside
But she's screaming in despair from within.
The men want her just to have her on their sleeve; they'll exploit her and leave.
Oh yeah, she thinks sarcastically, *It's a real blessing to be pretty.*

Fuck You

Fuck all you posers who think you're hard core.
You grew up middle class with two supportive parents but you claim you've got it rough and grew up poor.
You're not tough because you run your mouth, wear your pants low and walk with a fake limp,
Did you forget? We grew up in the same small town and I know you were never a thug, you were always a wimp.
Give it up buddy; lose the du rag and the ghetto slang because everyone can see
You're talking like you're black but you're whiter than me.

Observe my home town's courthouse and you'd see the same people each week.
Talking tough, bragging about crimes, not the least bit discreet.
To them it's a joke, a social scene for wannabes to meet.

Fuck you politicians and your politics
You make me sick. You talk shit but when it comes to a serious issue you passively sit without even attempting to deal with it.

Fuck the authorities who act like they're superior to the minority and think they're better than us because they have more seniority, more credibility, or more money.
Your speeches are redundant, your behaviour is repugnant, and your jokes aren't funny.

Fuck all the men who act sweet and then beat their girlfriends on the street.
Fuck the big guys who power trip because of their size.
Fuck the man who didn't realize I was a prize.

Fuck the guys who whistle at me on the street like I'm a piece of meat.
It's offensive and degrading, not flattering or sweet.
Even if my outfit is slightly revealing doesn't mean you'll ever be feeling me up, picking me up, or getting a touch of what's underneath.

Fuck the girls who have talked shit behind my back because I've got what they lack
Or because they didn't go through the shit I went through.
Fuck him, fuck her, and fuck you.
Fuck all the people who disrespect me and then expect me to just sit back and take that.

Fuck every guy that I've shot down who went around town and said he slept with me, said he passed me around.
If you even tried to kiss me I'd head butt you to the ground.
Sit down you overconfident, underdeveloped, cocky, sexist clown.

Fuck the rumours, fuck the glares,
Fuck the expectations and judgmental stares.

Fuck the police who charged me for weed at fifteen but allowed *a certain adult in my life to give it to me.*
He was supposed to protect me; instead he contributed to my juvenile delinquency.

He had no consequences. I was charged and he walked free.
Fuck the police who waste their time on a kid with a tiny amount of weed while pedophiles lurk the streets.

Fuck anyone who underestimates me.
No one knows the power that is in me.
And I am powerful.
But I have a form of power that has gone untold.
It isn't in the form of huge muscles,
It isn't in the form of money or material assets; it is deep within my soul.
I, as one girl have the power to contribute in this huge world.
So fuck anyone who doesn't take me seriously
If anyone tries to prevent me from accomplishing my purpose, I'll fight them fiercely.

Fuck you, fuck you, and fuck you.
Fuck all the guys who can beat me up to make themselves feel tough but when next to someone their size, they don't know what to do.

Hey dad – In my view,
You're a poser too.
Fuck you.
In my opinion, you've always been the fakest one I knew.
Do you feel like a man now?
In case you're wondering, I'm still standing somehow.
So hang your head in shame, while I take a bow.

Fuck anyone who thinks they know me when they have no clue about what I've been through.
And fuck all those who deny what is true.

I can't contemplate why our human race tries to complicate fate with lies and hate.
What's a girl to do?
Stand up and say FUCK YOU!

Blessed to Reach Adulthood

All the dangerous things I've done and high risk places I've been,
I'm surprised I've made it to eighteen.
I never thought certain things would happen to me.
I lived an extremely high risk life style and I thought I knew it all for a while
But I was just a lost little girl with a pretty smile.
I never thought of the possible outcome.
I just wanted to be accepted and have fun.
If I keep it up, I won't reach twenty-one.
It's time to be responsible and smart,
It's time for a fresh start.
My life could have been cut short so many times, any minute it could.
Today, if nothing else, I'm blessed to have reached adulthood.

"Some people are monsters and the
monsters sleep peacefully.
The peaceful people can't sleep at all,
haunted by monstrous memories."

Chapter 4

Justifiable Anger & P.T.S.D (Post Traumatic Stress Disorder)

Reality Check

I am deep and insightful. I have skills and potential.
I'm intelligent and creative; I could make a difference in this world
Through my writing, my ideas and with my empathy.
I could be a dedicated social worker or I could run a shelter for abused women and children, helping them cope on their transition journey.
I have compassion for children, animals, addicts, the abused; I've even had compassion for the *abuser*.
I have the brains and ideas for change- hey, I could be Prime Minister.
I could help evolve society by facing issues and investigating what led to them.
I could do anything, but no,
It all depends on income
What family, what area, and what class I'm born in.

In our society, you have to follow a certain curriculum.
You must complete elementary school, then high school, and then pay thousands of dollars for more school.
School's the only learning tool we validate but I learned all my lessons in a much harder way and school couldn't prepare me for what I would face.
Although I have the passion to help others and the life experience it requires, plus the desire to succeed,
The only way I'll qualify is if I pay with symbolic paper we call money and achieve a piece of paper that symbolizes a degree.
That's reality.

Reality is that in society the highest paying jobs are being a stripper, a prostitute or a criminal
Not a life-saving fire fighter, not a nurse tending to the ill.
And these occupations are the only ones with no requirement of previous education or skill.
If you don't have an education, connections or options and if you need money,
The quickest ever present option is one of these -
That's reality.

Reality is that respect isn't given to those who overcome hardships and do what is right.
It's given to the men with muscles, the one who can fight.
It starts on the school yard and continues in life.
People never insult him, he never has to watch his back or be afraid,
The big guys have got it made.
People won't try to mess with him, they won't even disagree.
This is reality.
They'll follow him around, behind him they'll trail.
He is the alpha male.
Being intimidating or being famous or rich are what gains people power and respect;
That's reality; the reality I've come to accept.

I am prey.
I will struggle every day, but they -
The big guys, celebrities and those who are rich,
They will have their asses kissed every day.
That's the reality of life and life's a bitch, if I dare say.

Reality is that to be a kind, caring young woman is not a blessing, but a punishment.
People will not take you seriously; they'll think nothing of violating you and fear no consequence.
You won't stand a chance.
The most frustrating part of all of this, the part that makes me sick, that makes me want to cry,
Is that if I want to be taken seriously; if I want them to think twice before fucking with me
My only chance is if I stand beside one of those big guys.
If I'm with him, they'll look at me different, and I'm not a target, I'm safe.
That's what is most frustrating, that's what I hate.
So, that frustrated and angry girl who has always been prey
Will be walked all over and she'll take it every day.
Strangers will target her, friends will misuse her and men will abuse her because "What's she going to do?"
That's reality, the reality I've seen as true.

Although I have so much rage and nothing to lose and although I'm so angry,
I'll never be feared, never be intimidating or even taken seriously.
Everyone will think they can walk all over me without consequences and they will without thinking twice-
That's the reality that is my life.

But in the long run, reality is that that girl will only be able to take so much before she snaps
And when she snaps, she'll be so dangerous because she's had to take so much crap.

And in order to prove a point, she'll have to go to the extreme;
She'll really have to make a statement just to get them to see.

Reality is that the tough guys are only viewed as tough because of their size and their act
But muscle mass decreases with age and that's a fact.
And the tough guys who fight the girl half their size, are only so tough until up against another whose muscles compare
And for every big guy, there's a bigger guy out there.

The most powerful and dangerous of all
Is really that soft spoken, underestimated girl
Because she has always had to fight and because she has so much rage from being made to feel like prey in a beasts world.

And she isn't faking it; she isn't just trying to look tough.
She really can't take it anymore, she's truly had enough.
So when she loses it and steps up to him she'll win
Because he's drunk and she's sober,
He's underestimating her but she knows if she makes one wrong move it's all over.
But he's not scared; he thinks it's a joke so he doesn't see it coming.
One shot in one spot and that's all it takes.

She has become the most dangerous, the most powerful and feared.
The one who was prey, who was robbed of everything, who shed the most tears, she has no fear.
She was ruined by the big tough guy

And has become the most dangerous of all,
Only her coldness is a lie.
She has to fake hate to be spared of her fate as prey
In the reality that has been her life.

You're so in denial You Probably Don't Think this Poem is about You
(*Inspired by the song *You're so vain* by Carly Simon)

You walk around like you're a tough guy but unless there was someone there to impress, someone could harm your own child and you'd just sit by.
No one from your past is still around and it's no wonder why. Countless friends, your ex-wife, your children; Keep telling yourself it's everyone else's fault while you deny, deny, deny. My whole life you kept going from partner to partner, to partner to partner, and…
Although every word I say is true you're so in denial you probably don't think this poem is about you, do you?

I used to want you in my life when I was young and naïve,
But I see through you now and there's not one of your lies that I believe.
Actions speak louder than words and you never acted like you cared about me.
You're a hypocrite and a coward but it's not me, it's yourself who you deceive.
I don't buy one lie and I'm not sipping whatever's in your coffee and…
Despite everything you have put me through you probably don't think this poem is about you, do you?

Well I hear you're an MMA fighter, there was a push up contest and you naturally won.

And you act like a biker, but you've never owned a motorcycle and even after stealing all my parts you still don't even have one.

And I hear you've stepped up for *someone else's* daughter and her son; how admirable.

Ask me how much respect I have for you; the answer is none.

I guess some people don't change in the end.

You have no morals or character, we all knew that when you hooked up with the wife of a close friend, and…

I feel sorry for anyone who doubts me and believes you, to the one who believes he's good and his words are true, you're so oblivious, you probably don't think this line is about you, do you?

Homicidal Princess

A homicidal princess
Seeking vigilante justice.
I gave you fair warning when I said I wouldn't be fucked with
Perhaps now you will accept this.

Like the others you didn't take me seriously.
Now do you believe it's not a joke when you fuck with me?
I told you I wouldn't take it. Now I have to show you; I'll make you see.

So, when you're literally on your knees and you're crying
And you can't sleep at night when you're trying,
Know it's because
You fucked with one that I love.

I won't be pushed around, won't have some clown play games with my head,
I gave you fair warning when I said, "Hurt one I love and you'll wish you were dead".
You deserve everything you get and I could have done so much more.
Be grateful I don't call cops; be grateful I let you walk out the door.

You proved you have no honour, no respect, no integrity; I will never look at you the same.
If you ever see me again you can hang your head in shame.

You think you're powerful? Now you just look lame.
I'm glad I saw your true colors because like the others, losing you was my gain.

I've just given you a taste; you still have no idea what it's like to have nothing.
Consider yourself lucky
Trust me,
When I say I can destroy you I'm not bluffing.

But I'll go about my life because I've proved my point and karma will make you fall.
It's clear you're not my soul mate; the devil owns your soul
And one by one, he will take it all.
I saw through your lies.
I sense the evil.
It can't be disguised,
I can see it in your eyes.

You have met your match –
Only I'm better than you because I have what you lack.
I have heart, I have soul, I have my freedom and I'm not giving it back.
I let you live so that you will always regret *the day that you fucked with my cat.*

Call me crazy,
I've just adapted to survive in this patriarchal society of greed and vanity.
Yeah, it's true what you've heard
But it's because of men like you if I'm disturbed.

You didn't know who you were fucking with but now you'll never forget.
I'm so much smarter and stronger than when we met.
Far from helpless,
I'm a homicidal princess.

Trust Issues

He's still a part of me.
It's no longer innocently.
He haunts my nightmares and steals my dreams.
It affects my days.
His ego demands his ways.

And where's dad when you need him?
I'm hurt yet plead with him.
Then another man looks at me,
I guard myself, it comes naturally
Is any man capable of being my friend?
Will any man not hurt me in the end?

Nightmares

Even if you leave him in real life, even if you run away;
They always find you in your nightmares, and disturbing vivid nightmares can ruin your entire day.
I'm never free,
He will always haunt me and in my nightmares he can always find me.

Nightmares- there I'm even more helpless than in reality.
I'm stuck standing still when I'm trying to run, my voice a whisper when I'm trying to scream.
I dread sleep. There's no peace.
So, I try to stay awake,
But eventually my body shuts down, there's only so much the body can take.
Then, while I sleep; I sweat, I scream, I shake.
They're so vivid and real,
I relive the feelings I don't want to feel.
When I wake up, the nightmare doesn't end,
Instead reality is a continuous extension.

No one can help me and I'm a target.
No one has loved me and people are heartless.
It wasn't a dream, I know by the permanent injuries, the scars, and the cuts on my wrists.
The monster does exist.
There may not be a monster under the bed
But there is a monster in my head,

Haunting me and taunting me, memories of the cruel words he said.

Some people are monsters and the monsters sleep peacefully. The peaceful people can't sleep at all, haunted by monstrous memories.
Just when I think it can't get any more unfair,
I try to rest my head in hopes of a new, better day and am bombarded by yet another nightmare.

"Anger is justifiable
When there is no justice in an angry world."

Chapter 5
Grief & Self Harm

Self-Sabotage

What am I trying to accomplish?
Am I trying to be my perpetrators accomplice?
Do I have a death wish?
The rage is constant
And I don't want it but I can't stop it.

Sadness & Pain

If you see sorrow in my eyes and if when you look at me it seems I could cry,
If my voice shakes and you sense my heart ache,
If I never seem truly happy
Know it's not you, it's me.
Know it's not self-pity; it's grief for my murdered baby,
Regret for the dreams I buried,
Anger toward the man my poor mother married.
Its pain from childhood attacks which led to the loss of things I can never get back
And choices I can't retract.

My heart aches
For the good people who never get a break,
Like the abused, the addicts, the poor, the sick, the strays.

I actually consider it abnormal to be entirely happy
When there are countless others who are still struggling.
To better our world, to better our people is key.
We must evolve spiritually.

Anger is justifiable
When there is no justice in an angry world.

The rich get rich and the poor get poorer;
Perhaps this is because those who possess the majority of the wealth are greedy.

Yet, to the contrary, gentle souls give their all and therefore may become needy.

Learned helplessness is what to expect when one is constantly experiencing an attack
But is never able to fight back.
If you sense the sadness or the rage, attribute it to empathetic heart ache,
Personal grief and a unique deep sensitivity
How can I be okay?
The memories of yesterday still haunt me today.

The Cutter

I cut myself to see if I still feel.
I'm numb.
I cut myself to see if I am real.
What have I become?
They can't see my pain so they minimize it.
They can't see the demons inside.
It seems no one empathizes.
Internally, the scars hide.

I cut myself so I don't kill him and him and him.
I spare them and take my rage out on myself.
They should be thankful.
I cut myself because pain is what's familiar; I can't imagine anything else.

I cut myself to control the unrelenting, overwhelming pain.
I cut for the rage, humiliation, degradation, injustices and shame.
I put the pipe to my mouth, the bottle to my lips,
I put the knife to my arm,
And I go to a bar and strip.
Always to escape
And it's always a mistake.

July 5, 2009

I was blessed with the gift of life on this day.
I drove my car into a ravine and walked away.
I was taking the wrong road in life so I drove off it – literally.
The fact that I survived, uninjured at that, was a miracle and it should have been a wake-up call for me.
It's quite the life I lead. I want to be the person I'm meant to be,
But it's spinning out of control like the car rolled and it's too late for me.
I need to stop my old ways to end the dark days,
But I see no other way.

"I have so much sadness, anger, guilt, shame, and pain. I see such beauty in the world and I know I am meant to be good, but there is a strong dark force; a deep, dark, demonic presence that tempts me and entraps me."

Chapter 6
The Addict & the Desire to Escape

Crack Cocaine

I toke,
Exhale smoke
Different than anything tasted before.
It opened the door
To more and more and more –
And more and more and more and more.

Nauseous, delightfully toxic, empty energy.
Mixed, mumbled, misunderstood, whispered words screamed.
All in a matter of seconds
And then regrets, nothing left, so tired, wired, weak
Desperate for one more peak and then- repeat, repeat, repeat.

Chasing a dragon in a fairy tale, chasing something that's not there, not real.
Falling in the darkness and she doesn't care because the darkness has its appeal.
And when she dies, N.H.I
No Humans Involved is what they'll write.

All her countless gifts, amazing qualities, all the possibilities
Could have been forgotten and gone to waste as a result of just one taste.
Would you put a gun to your mouth and pull the trigger?
It's a game of Russian roulette and the pipe is the gun but its destruction is even deeper and bigger.
Why risk it?
Don't become a statistic.
If you're struggling and need help, admit it.

Lost in the Garden of Eden

I was tempted by the forbidden and persuaded by the serpent.
I didn't see the harm, I didn't mean to sin.
I wanted to escape, I wanted freedom.
Now I'm trapped in the Garden of Eden.
It seemed so unfair.
Why was this tree there?
If the fruit it grew caused suffering and despair?

Was it a test? Was I set up to fail?
Is that why God gave us free will?
Was he laughing at me?
Where is he?
I feel so distant and I need him.
I'm lost and alone in the Garden of Eden.

I feel so ashamed and foolish for my mistake.
I have sinned and fear what will become of my fate.
Ever since then, it's been dark and cold in the garden.
I'm scared, naked and alone
And the anger is making my soft spirit harden.
Negative energy has overpowered me and I fear the demons.
The devil is real I've seen him.
He lives with me here, in the Garden of Eden.

"I was lured to the place with the
dim lights and late nights.
The place with the endless supply
Of whatever you needed to die."

Chapter 7
The Stripper & the Desire to be Wealthy and Have Money

Desperation

Help me,
Why do I continuously leave the path I'm on when I'm just beginning to feel at peace and am surrounded by beauty, to surround myself with negative people, places and things?
Money – pieces of paper, symbolic power, the dirtiest substance in the world.
What costs will I pay to pay the cost of my dreams?
I'm disgusted by what I've heard, what I've seen, where I was and what I've been.
A heart shattered.
Good intentions no longer matter.
Strangers see my smile and to them I may even appear care free,
I walk with fake confidence and most believe.
A spirit crushed and weak,
Still I long to learn what I'm meant to teach.

It Drains my Soul

The money is not worth the guilty conscience.
The satisfaction of taking action and giving him a ruthless reaction is not worth the consequence.
All the money in the world is not worth causing my mom and brother heart ache and shame. Getting quick money isn't worth what it takes.
I take their money but what do they take from me?
They take the only thing I have left: my dignity.
The darkness deepens depression.
Excessive amounts of alcohol increases each impulse and leads to my regression.
Portraying myself as something I'm not, portraying myself as so much less.
Portraying myself as the character I created, until there's no sign of the real me left.
It takes its toll,
It drains my soul.

Objectified

My pretty lace shirt falls to the dirt symbolizing the mistreatment and the hurt.
My valuable skirt tossed aside, representing my pride,
And as I stand naked and my panties hit the floor
I know I've lost it all, can't lose anymore
Pride or respect.
What did I expect?
They only see my body. They don't see me as a whole.
When they only see my body they strip me of my soul.
All eyes are on me, yet no one can see *me*.
They see parts-
Parts of whomever my name that night may be.

The Devil's Dungeon

I was lured to the place with the dim lights and late nights.
The place with the endless supply
Of whatever you needed to die.

I got lost in the darkness.
I got lost in a place as dark as the souls within it.
A place where neither sunlight nor time exist
And only few who get in make it out of it.

It drains souls and destroys girls.
It attracts the evil and tempts the weak.
The weak are easy prey and so the evil feast.
Common characteristics: sin and deceit.
Yet every night people come in and waste away in the devil's dungeon.

The alcoholic, now old and alone, makes the devil's dungeon his home
Even though he knows the friendship is fraudulent and she knows it's wrong,
The devil's dungeon is the only place anyone with a twenty dollar bill belongs
And anyone can have a girlfriend for the length of a song.

He pays for companionship.
He makes her sick.
He loves the companionship.
She can't stomach it.

It's a place where one with a conscience cannot survive
But evil narcissistic predators thrive.
It's a jungle and they'll eat you alive.

She exploits him, taking him for all he has and laughing behind his back.
He exploits her, taking advantage of her desperate situation, offering what she lacks.
There's a power imbalance and a constant flow of negative energy.
She has what he wants and he has what she needs.
In the jungle, she's wounded prey and the hungry lions feed.

She's treated like an object and is dehumanized.
Yet she tolerates it and she takes it,
She puts on a pretty smile and she fakes it
Because a long time ago she realized,
I might as well get paid; I'm sexualized and objectified every day anyway.
No, it didn't start here and it won't end here.
Even if she escapes the dungeon there are still demons to fear;
They're everywhere.

Forgotten daughters, faceless females answer to false names.
They all participated in her demise but when she's destroyed it's her they'll blame.
She never stood a chance
An angel lost in the devil's maze.

I kept crawling out of the darkness only to discover no light in sight.

Lifeless and numb,
I was unable to fight.
I went back to the devil's dungeon
The place I was lured to and now couldn't escape from.

He's ashamed to be there and so is she.
She's the one who is judged but he's just as guilty.
She was desperate, discouraged and afraid,
But him; the wealthy business man, he had it made.

They block out their daughters and wives but they're forced to recognize their hypocritical lives when they look into her eyes.
Yet, they walk away in their drunken state and remember nothing she said the next day.
She put a spell on them
But it wasn't enough.
She thought she reached their heart and got through to their soul.
She thought they saw her differently after listening to the story she told
But she does not have the ability to warm hearts so cold.

Rescued & Destroyed

I had lost hope.
I was trying to numb emotions to cope.
Such bright eyes tried to hide my soul and look dark and cold.
Just a young woman but I felt so old.
There seemed no reason to write, no reason to put up a fight.
I was drained.
Life was meaningless and cruel, each day the same.
Man drove me mad.
I was robbed of everything I had.
Stuck in a cycle and spinning out of control.
I was spinning myself into a deep hole.
Every day was so dark and loud.
I was humiliated and degraded but I just wanted to feel loved and be proud.
I was never who I answered to;
She was merely who I believed I needed to be
A character conceived,
But I was never my stage name, I was always me.
Then, a wannabe hero arrived on the scene and it seemed he was straight out of a dream.
Everything was fairy-tale like and serene.
But the dream became a nightmare and my hero my destroyer,
Held hostage in the fake fairy tale that wouldn't have a happily ever after, and it seemed it would never be over.
If he was sent to me for a purpose, he served that purpose when I got out of the satanic circus

But he wouldn't let me go, because of ego he was convinced I was now his own and he couldn't admit that he'd been outgrown.

But as time progressed so did I and he quickly lost appeal in my eyes because he was just like the rest of them.

I should have known there were no heroes, only evil omens in the devil's dungeon.

Chapter 8
Desperate Pleas & Words of Warning

Society's Double Standards

First, allow each verse to hit you like a curse.
Know we can't reverse this diverse universe
It just hurts how we continue to make it worse.

In a world where we are so critical it's typical to overlook a hypocritical criminal
But each criminal committed a crime for a reason and now look at the situation he's in.
Many politicians are criminals committing treason
But they don't have to pay,
So we send the message that, for some people doing what's wrong is okay.
We target the crimes in the ghettos
But we look the other way when they're committed by the government, the police, the judge or the C.E.O.

We must ignore the diversions
Unless we're sure they're urgent.
We must bring an emergence
Of honest, proud people and to do this we must be an honourable person.
This world is magical and radical, vast and great.
Let's stop the ignorance and hate before it's too late.

If you live for the wealth or live for the fame,
If you're concerned about how you look to others,
Chances are you're suppressing insecurities or shame.
Eventually you'll be old and have to retire from the game
And you'll still require fulfillment but will have limited opportunities to gain.

Which Pair of Shoes Should I Buy?

Every minute, people suffer and children die,
In the meantime, we're trying to decide which pair of shoes to buy.
Products are tested on animals, strays wonder the streets, and abused pets are kicked
While we're still wondering which color to pick.
A man beats his wife, a mother fears for her children's life,
Listening to his excuse this time with tears and sighs,
And our biggest dilemma is, "Do they come in my size?"
Big companies use slave labour and underpaid employees have no rights
And when we buy their products we're endorsing it, so how do we sleep at night?
We could buy fair trade but we don't even try
We're consumers; we just buy, buy, buy!
We have the money to so we'll consume, consume, consume; we don't care about you.

When single parent's struggle to feed their kids and telling their children it's going to be alright is a lie,
Keep thinking of yourself and which shoes you should buy.
Then walk outside and ignore the homeless man with the sign.
Step over the woman sleeping on the street; keep telling yourself *they're* burdens on society.
But the next time you're trying to decide which pair of shoes to buy,

Think of the barefooted children and all the struggling men and women
If you can afford new shoes for every occasion, you can afford to make a donation.

Life is Killing Me

I really hate this life;
I love and appreciate the amazing potential it has
But I hate the reality of how it is.

I've watched my mom always work hard and do what is right and sacrifice.
She didn't give in to temptation; she's always been the bigger person.
She has never lost faith and is always able to find the positive and today
She has to fight for what she's entitled to and she continues to struggle although she deserves a break.
She is underestimated and underappreciated.

I've watched my brother always be transparent, real and honest and never conform to the norm.
He has always been true to himself.
He has always been respectful and modest.
Like our mom, he is selfless and has sacrificed.

They say nice guys finish last
But maybe it's because there are not enough good guys in the race
And there are too many "bad boys" to chase.
Being so evolved and having such values, practicing strong willpower and self-discipline, he does no harm and rarely does wrong.

With everything going for him, his biggest problem is it seems he doesn't belong.
Well,
Who wants to?

This is not to put them down,
They need not feel ashamed.
This reality doesn't reflect poorly on them,
It's life I hate; its life I blame.

I'm the impulsive one, the defiant one, the one who acts out and rebels.
I wish I was as self-disciplined as my brother and as forgiving as my mother
Because I can't just sit back and watch as life as we know it is hell.

The reality of this life is killing me.
It's driving me crazy
Making me numb, changing who I am, making me fear what I've become.
Haunting and taunting me,
It's making me sick
Literally weakening my immune system,
Life is causing my death.

Youth Lost

Amber alerts, foster care, drugs, hitch hiking and hand cuffs at thirteen.
A stolen car, robberies and B&E, holding cells, a group home, and probation at fifteen.
Pregnant by her first real boyfriend at eighteen,
Followed by a brutal assault causing a miscarriage and crime scene.
She hid his drugs and advocated for him at sentencing.
She stood by him and was sure he'd change because of a fake apology
She was deceived.
Pimped out by friends of father,
He should have protected her but didn't bother.
At twenty, thought she met the man of her dreams,
Followed by arms pinned down by his knees, a shattered hand and wrist, and reconstructive surgery.
Serious drug addictions, serious loss of ambitions, self-harm and homicidal ideation.
Then, on impulse, she drives her car into a ravine and somehow finds herself in an even worse situation.
Rights infringed and then after everything, she's deemed guilty while never having an attorney or legal representation.
The court may label her a criminal; if that's what she's become the same court is responsible for the creation.
Treatment centers, women shelters and inadequate/unsafe housing,
Professionals who are supposed to be helping are sitting on their asses lounging.

Desperate to be protected, met a man who it seemed would provide this.
Trafficked and sold like an object
He preyed on her like it was his home-work project.
Trying to pick up all the pieces, totally alone and living in fear
Now it's a new year and she's reflecting on where she's been and where she is, wondering where to go from here?

"Supportive" Housing

Women, children, pets.
Countless incompetent, unprofessional security guards,
Ambulances and cop cars,
Drug users and their guests.
Crack pipes, needles and razor blades,
I was never told it would be this way;
I was told it would be safe.
Rape, prostitution and bleeding,
Crying and screaming and pleading.
Afraid to go out, afraid to stay in,
Damned if I do, damned if I don't,
I can't win.
Inconsistencies, false promises and ever changing staff.
Harm reduction for who? I don't know whether to cry or to laugh.
Unrealistic expectations,
Triggers and temptations.
Years of my life pass as the clock ticks
And I wonder how many more setbacks I'll have to deal with.
They could have helped me become a success story
But it's too late.
I couldn't just sit around and wait
I'm still yet to hear and explaination or hear a "We're sorry".
Stigmatized and dehumanized,
Invalidated and unheard.
I've survived and now I'll thrive sharing my experiences through the written word.

Love Lies

Love is a person's desire
Nothing more, nothing I require.
It has made me weak and tired
It is not something I seek or that is of dire need.

Love I will never admire.
Love is a liar.
His love will expire and I'll be left alone to put out its fire.
Furious flames of passionate pleasure so pure.
Love is a disease and there is no cure.
Love is not what it once was and we are not what we once were.

Most men who say they love me, lie.
Each time it hurts my pride.
If I think I'm falling in love I should hide.
There have been times I tried.
I pushed him away, I ran away, but he wouldn't let me go and he pried.
Eventually I gave in only to be hurt again.

I once thought,
You are my soul mate;
Without my mate
I am merely a lonely soul.
But I forgot,
I'm an individual
And even when we're apart,

I'm perfectly whole.

If one loves me, let that love be relieved
Release it and set me free.
An equal love can never be received.
A good woman, now more confused than before, again will be deceived.
A mutual understanding of love is not perceived or agreed.

The phrase, *I love you* has become a threat.
Falling in love is something I regret.
I love you means nothing to me.
How could he love me and be so mean?
How could he look into my eyes and call me names as he screams?
Is that how love is supposed to be?
Love has cost me everything.
Please, don't love me.

Malicious and vicious was his kiss more punishment than bliss so how the fuck could love exist?
He hated me, degraded me, humiliated me and jaded me.
I was deprived of my pride when he laughed as I cried.
It was then I realized
I need to abstain,
I need to refrain from the game that brings only pain.
The game that men play that makes my heart decay,
It's a battle I won't fight, a game I won't play.

Men pretend you can depend on them
But love to me is absurd,
No more than a word,

Love to me is disturbed.
Love is stupidity, love is pain.
Love is a loss, not a gain.
It's a ruthless game that brings with it shame.
Love is as unpredictable as a fire's flame.
Love is always wild, never tame.

Love is weakness; love is superficial, conditional, and fake.
It leads to heartache and is followed by heart break.
I will give, love will take.
It's a foolish mistake.
Romantic love is not in my fate.

It's out of question, out of reach.
It's valuable how much a destroyed love can teach.
I'll never want it, need it, ask or beseech.
Love leads to disappointment and dependency.
With romantic, conventional, "man and wife" love, I do not agree.
Non attachment, I will preach.

"Man and wife".
It's said in a way that she becomes an extension of him in life.
And the father "gives her away", then she takes her husband's name?
What about her can remain the same?
Love is lame.

Life Can Go Either Way

One life,
Multiple paths,
Which way to go?
The mind is polluted,
Life is convoluted,
So much is going to waste.
The body shakes, the heart aches, all you see is death and decay.
Lost in concrete jungles, trying not to stumble, skies are dark and grey.

The mind flourished, the planet is nourished, people love, share and pray.
Surrounded by beauty and peace, children laugh and play.
It's a beautiful day.
Multiple paths,
One life,
The darkness and the light,
Life could go either way.

Fantasy Land

There is a fantasy land, where people believe what they want to believe, see what they want to see and hear what they want to hear.
Its people like these who claim to shed no tears and have no fear.
Winter is warm, summer is cold,
You pick one age and never grow old.
You don't acknowledge or take responsibility for past mistakes.
You just say, "I don't want to hear any negative crap from the past" and that's all it takes.
It's a fantasy world where ignorance is bliss and your entire identity is fake.
I've been there before and I never want to go back to that place.
You believe lies are true, you didn't do anything wrong and no one should be upset with you.
Now that I think about it, I kind of understand why the people who live there don't want to move.
It takes a strong person to accept responsibility for all that they have put you through.

If I Lose my Mind

If I lose my mind,
If I can no longer define
That line
Between what's wrong and what's right;
If something happens to me tonight,
God knows I put up a good fight.

I'm waiting for karma, up every night waiting for its arrival,
Waiting for it to visit the monster who terrorized me – the unwilling rival.
Until then, somehow I keep going through the motions, suppressing explosions of emotions.
Meditation, creation, and positive visualization using my imagination all combined are part of my powerful pleasant potion.
Those of us who walk this earth are the chosen.

Untitled

This world is not as pleasant as it could be.
We all want to be happy, to feel loved and live free
But it's not that easy.
With a body and a life comes responsibility.
We must remain humble and we must accept many things.
Even a princess cries and even a Priest dies.
Accept the outcast and accept your own past.
To hurt or insult another is like damaging the Creator's magnificent art work.
We must look deeper than the surface. Each being is perfectly imperfect.
We must appreciate the unique abilities and talents we each hold.
A wasted talent is one that is not utilized and goes forever untold.

Adapt to Survive

There was a time I dreamed of being a wife and mother,
Only his and with no other;
This is what I once believed I was born to be.
But tragically, it's too late for me and I no longer have the ability.
My womanhood was robbed from me at eighteen, so I adapted accordingly.

All I've gained aside from pain is that lesson that remains the same.
Do not seek protection from another,
Become *your own* protector.
Live to honour your mother and your brother.

I see through men, women, people.
There is not about to be a sequel of a continuous story starring me as the unequal.
I'm this age and I've never been loved.
It became a nightmare and now just isn't something I dream of.

I'm just not compatible.
There is no simpatico.
If I'm strong I'll let him go.
I won't fear the tears that flow.
I am the one meant to be solo.

I am worthy of the same treatment he expects,
But it seems there is no mutual respect left.
So excuse me while I withdraw, rebel, and regress.

"Silently soul search, seeking simplicity.
Suspicions spirit sucking sinners
solicit soldiers skilfully.
Shameful sorrow suddenly swallows strongest species.
So, strong soldiers succumb, suddenly shady
shapeless shadows standing still, silently shaking."

Chapter 9

Tongue Twisting Truth & Word Play

Words within Words

I avoid
A void.
I run away
From a way
That's different.
They're never there.
I know I should say no.
I'm amazed
By a maze
Of red tape.
Is it a disease?
Or is it my dis-ease
With reality?
It is
What it is.
Less power:
Powerless.
Less help:
Helpless.

Tongue Twisting Truth

Action.
Adverse attractions.
Assertive attitude, automatically assumed
And all acquaintances agree
Anger, anguish, agony, and animosity are all adapted appropriately.
All aimed at anyone awaiting an attack.
As assailants are afforded all advice and amends,
Abandoned angels abide and accept abuse and are ashamed as adolescents.
All awaiting anyone advocating against an aggressor; an assailant.

But batterers become badder because bigot, big shot, barrister bastards battle bluffing.
Black becomes blacker.
Brutally beat, battling beyond belief.
Broken bones, brainwashed, bedevilment, brain cells blown.
Blatantly bitter but beautifully blossoming, becoming better.
Broken bond beyond bettering became blackened by blame.

Closet criminals con carefully,
Consciously, convincingly
Cultivating, calculating.
Consequently capturing convenient characters carefully conceived.
Changing, contradictory character confined.
Crazy, careless, cocky, cruel combined.

Created confusion challenged
Can cause complainant concerning consequence.
Choices considered consistent considering complainant's conscience-
Complex corruption constant.

Dark deeds dismissed.
Degraded, discouraged, defeated, depressed.
Discovering dominant demons.
Defensive, determined.
Daring, deadly, defiant.
Destructive detrimental damage doesn't destroy delicate daughters.
Dead-beat dad's direct disrespect denying daughters does, disproportionately.
Dishonourable dictators destroying.
Damsel's distress doubled,
Distracted, dismissed discrepancies.

Enemies exist everywhere embodying everything.
Elusive, empty explanations, excuses, expectations.
Energize, examine enemy's eyes.
Embrace enlightenment, enter euphoria, evaluate ethics.
Explosive emotions, exciting excursions, everything's extreme, everything's excessive.
Enormous ego enlivened evil,
Evil enhanced, everyone's entranced.

Fight fiercely for freedom, fight for fairness.
Forgive, forget frivolous fuss.
Follow former feminists, form fellowships, fearlessly flash fists.

Finally, forbid foulness, forsake false fate, focus.
Foresee future fake friendships; finish forthright, free from further feelings fundamentally ferocious.

Gradually gaining grounded greatness,
Gently generating good.
God gives great gifts.
Give gratitude.
Generations grow, guardian Godsends glow.
Giving guidance granted graciously, God's girl genuinely grew.
Greedy governments grovel guilty.
Go gather guilty gripping God's golden gate.
Genuine genius generalized, getting glares, girlhood gone graduates.

Hungry hunters, hunting helpless.
Harmful, hot headed, horrible, heartless.
Holding her hostage, harassing her.
Her heart hurts. Hourly humiliation haunts her.

Immediate image impressive in its intelligence
I ignored Immanent Indicators, indulged in imaginary ideals, incredibly intense.
Impetuous.
Impatient.
Inconsiderate.
Inconsistent information.
Insults, injuries, increased Insecurities.
Injustices.
Insane insinuations invade innocence.
Improper, inadequate investigations.

Ignorant, insensitive investigator is incompetent.
I'm increasingly impatient.

January's joyless journey.
Jealousy Junkie.
Justice.
Just joking.

Killers killing, kidnappers kidnapping.
Karma kills killers.
Knowledge kept kin kind.

Learning lessons, lessons learned later left legends.
Legacy lasts, lengthening long line.
Little lives legitimized.
Learned lessons, losses lessen.

My message misconstrued, meaning merely mused.
Meditation's my medication.
Mystical magical miracles mesmerize me.
Mature master mind make me millions.
My Mother: My mentor, my motivation.
Many misjudge me.
Maybe misjudgement might metaphorically mirror me.
My misconception?
Muscles make most men mean.

Nauseating nightmares, nervous nights, nonstop negativity.
Never negotiate naively.
Neglecting needs never nourishes nations,
Nevertheless, noxious, nonsensical nuclear noise numbs numerous nationalities.
No one notices new nonviolent notions now necessary.

Outspoken, oppressed, overlooked, objectified.
Oddly obliged.
Offended, overruled, opprobrious,
Overbearing, obnoxious.
Overpowered, overwhelmed, outraged.
Obscene obedience obtained.
Out of options?
Observe obscure optimists.
Outgrow old obsessive objectives.

Particular people promote prejudice;
Predominantly politicians, police, press.
Prematurely presumptuous. Patriarchal pricks.
Powerless people pray, pleading passionately.
Predators prowling, portraying pleasant personalities.
Princesses punished.
Private prisons prohibit prosperous possibilities.
Progress passed past problems
Patiently practicing personal pendulum
Pondering powerful phenomenon.

Quite questionable qualities quicken quietly.
Qualified Queen quivering.

Reasonable rage.
Residual resentment radiates.
Release rage, release rejection, relieve resentment.
Rejoice, renew, repent.
Receive righteous retribution.
Refuse relentless, reckless, ruthless reunions.

Silently search seeking simplicity.
Suspicious spirit sucking sinners solicit soldiers skilfully.

Shameful sorrow suddenly swallows strongest species.
So, strong soldiers succumb, suddenly shady shapeless shadows standing still, silently shaking.
Spiritual souls spoiled.
Strongest species self-sabotaged.

Terrible trivial temper tantrums,
Torture, terrorism.
Thorough threats trick thoughts.
Time ticks, tick-tock.
Topics too traumatic too talk.
Tears tell the twisted truth.
Tension thickens, then the tasteless, terrifying traditions.

Ultimate unconsciousness undoes universe.
Unconvinced unconsciousness unwanted.
Unhealthy urges uncontrollable,
Unrelenting, unspeakable urges unbearable.

Victorious Victorian Viking,
Violated viscously, ventures vigilantly.
Violent visuals, verbal vulgarities.

Who will welcome worn whimpering women?
Wishful with wisdom, wonderful wise words written,
When we women were wronged wicked witnessed.
XXX
X boyfriend
X rated
X-ray
Yesterday,
Zero zest

"I run from the bright darkness while standing still
And I use all of my effort to climb a flat hill.

Chapter 10
Oxymora & Metaphorical Symbolism

How Things Can Change

Darkness, danger, violence, forbidden,
Hopeless, fearful, hurt, hidden -
End.
Bright, safe, friendly, happy,
Hopeful, fearless, glee –
Beginning.
Oh, how quickly things can change.

Bright, safe, friendly, happy,
Hopeful, fearless, glee –
Beginning.
Darkness, danger, violence, forbidden,
Hopeless, fearful, hurt, hidden -
End.
Oh, how quickly things can change.

Good People have it Bad and Bad people have it Good

Bad people have it good.
They're rich from scheming and greed, a ruthless attitude and taking more than they need.
They're happy because they're lost in their own denial and are oblivious to or unaffected by all those who still suffer.
Often, they're beautiful because they rarely stress, they can afford proper nutrition and they are the abusers not the abused.
They seem at peace and sleep comfortably because they have no conscience and lack empathy.
They are successful because they are merciless and with a cut throat attitude they'll do whatever it takes to get ahead.
They'll lie, cheat, steal and sometimes they buy their success or everything is simply handed to them.
They seem charming and desirable because they lack authenticity and sincerity, they just tell you what you want to hear and they conceal their true colors, motives and intentions.
They're always surrounded by friends or loved ones because one by one as they burn their bridges with people, they quickly move on, replacing each of them.
They can do this because their hearts are cold and because they avoid taking accountability at all costs.
They're never alone because they're always using someone for something.
However, if they are alone, then they are in bad company and find themselves uncomfortable;

And now they've got it bad.
How quickly things can change.

Good people have it bad.
They're often poor because they were trusting and gave the benefit of the doubt time and time again but they were scammed each time or they're poor because they're giving and they have literally given the shirt off their back.
They often have poor health as a result of poverty or because they're the survivors, not the attackers.
They often can't sleep at night due to an innate awareness and empathy and are burdened by the world's tragedies.
They may struggle with addiction or mental health issues, such as anxiety or depression or they were the victimized, not the victimizer, and this combined with the awareness of world tragedies can lead to the need to escape.
They may seem socially awkward, shy, or even odd because they're real, they don't put on a front or conform to the norm.
They are different and rare.
They may seem or be lonely because they are careful who they subject themselves to so they may find themselves with only a few friends or family members.
But they are not concerned with how many friends they have or how big their family is, they care about the *quality* of these relationships and their relationship with *themselves*.
They struggle because things weren't just handed to them, they're not overly aggressive, nor do they possess an egotistical sense of entitlement. They don't complain and they don't choose the easy way out.

They're often deprived and so, they are resourceful and they appreciate whatever they have,
And because they are the Good, on the Right Path, somehow the Universe provides them with exactly what they need
And because they don't find their happiness in materialistic, external things, they know even with nothing,
They still possess the most important things;
The biggest hearts of all, the wisest of souls, the most beautiful minds, and suddenly they find
They now have it good regardless.
How quickly things can change.

Poor people can still be rich and the richest man or woman can still be poor.
I do not wish to be rich in money. Why would I desire the dirtiest substance in the world?
Of course I wish to live comfortably and I *do* desire paper.
I desire to expose systemic injustices and worldwide corruption through the power of the written word
And so, I write my thoughts on paper
And that paper becomes priceless.

Without any money or assets I am still rich.
I'm rich in blessings, like the many second chances bestowed upon me.
I'm rich in family, even if this only consists of my mother and brother and no other.
I am rich in potential; all of the potential I individually possess.
I am rich in knowledge and wisdom from everything I've learned
And these lessons I must never forget.

Personal Paradox

Dare to be trusting,
Although trusting has led to being made a fool.
Dare to be loving and giving and kind
In a world that is cruel.

Dare to be content
Even when consumed by fear and grief.
Dare to smile
At every scowling stranger you meet.

Dare to laugh
At ridiculous, unfortunate circumstances.
Dare to give second chances.

No one and nothing can harden me.
The essence of my soul remains unchanged.
You can't change me.
My spirit will always remain the same.
And I would rather be used than use another, I'd rather be hurt than hurt another.
You can attack me, I will recover.
It's only if I join their game and inflict pain that I'll never be the same.
If they're determined to fight, let them.
I'll take it, I'll rise above it and I'll have a clear conscience at night.

It's better to be too trusting than to be cold.

I'd rather be too passive than too bold.
I'd rather be too giving than greedy.
I'd rather lose trying than win cheating.

I'd rather be heartbroken than cause another heart ache.
My positive qualities have become my negative traits
And although I'm suffering,
I suppose I prefer it this way.
If this shall be thy death of me,
I accept my fate.

Untitled

I fight peacefully,
And all of my life I've silently screamed.
I run from the bright darkness while standing still
And I use all of my effort to climb a flat hill.
I try to forget the soft tone of his harsh words.
Surrounded by millions I'm alone and what once seemed clear is now blurred and obscured.

Am I full of emptiness?
Those who do bad appear to have it so good
Isn't there something wrong with this?

Comfortable in my own discomfort,
Calm in chaos and crisis.
People tell lies so honestly,
I know it isn't supposed to be like this.

My strengths can become my weaknesses
Or I can be strong in the moment I am weak.
Even when I have nothing,
I still have everything I need.

Away from the Norm I Lean

Do not be fooled by the "norms" in society,

Do not follow them blindly.

Society's norms are the most abnormal things I've seen.

I followed along and the norm misguided me.

Now it's the other direction I lean.

Chapter 11
Reframing and Black & White Thinking

Bitter Sweet Reality

The darkness is not all I see.
I also see generosity and compassion, perhaps just not as frequently.
So I will do my best to contribute to making the screams from the world the music of my flute.
In the bad there's good and in the good there's bad.
If I'm happy and others are suffering, shouldn't I still be sad?

Summer Snowfall

For our love is as powerful as the heaviest rain.
It nourishes us as we blossom and cleanses us of past pain.
It is as deep as the ocean and as vast as the sky.
Like the most complex abstract painting there is more to it than meets the eye
Like the most magical, mystical moment, it's impossible to completely describe...
That's the way love is between you and I.

But our love is like a snowfall in summer- untimely.
Situations and circumstances prevent it's prevail and so many things remind me.
When I think of the times we laughed, I cry...
That's the way love is between you and I.

The Rose

A beautiful delicate rose loses its petals so gradually nobody knows.
Somehow, untouched beauty still shows.
The harsh wind takes another petal, another piece of the flower.
The weight of a single rain drop takes yet another and the rose, although resilient, is overpowered.

A single rose lost.
It grew between the weeds, blossomed in the cold, and grew into a flower without ever being a seed.

Gone with the wind, the rose petals drift
Until eventually, the rose as it was no longer exists.
It shed every layer that made it exactly how it is.
Now there is no trace of it.
It will not be remembered, it will not be missed.

Awaken to your Dream

Do you scream silently?
Do you see blindly?
Are you rushing to get nowhere?
Are you comfortably in despair?

I ran but remained in the same place.
I ran because I was afraid.
I was running from someone but I wasn't being chased.
I wanted to escape from me-
A monster, they had me believe.

I wept dry tears, felt painful pleasure,
Horrible happiness and soft pressure,
Insulting compliments and cruel love,
I was knowingly oblivious, a willing hostage, unwilling to accept this until I rose above.

I saw the light through the darkness.
I awoke to dream.
To find balance amidst the unbalanced and kindness in a world that can be so mean.

Part 2
The Light

Empowering Poetry & Survival Techniques

Introduction

Once Upon a Time
There was a girl who was full of potential.
She had a heart of gold, an ancient sagacious soul, the imagination of a philosopher, and a brilliant mind.
She possessed women's intuition even as a girl.
She was a dreamer and she dreamed of changing the world
And off into the big world she went, not knowing what she'd find.
She was seeking uncertain possibilities and against her mother's wishes she ventured through the world blind.
She was innocent, sweet and naïve.
She was a predator's dream.

All the human earth predators who came across her wanted to claim her for them to destroy,
But the alpha predator; the Spirit Devil forbade any one man or woman from claiming her life, she was his toy.
Out of his own immense, inhumane hatred, just because she was so good and pure hearted,
He wanted her to suffer more than any one man or woman could cause her.
So, the Devil put a curse on the girl and as soon as she came into this world it would have all started.
She would be surrounded by powerful earth predators everywhere she turned.
No one predator would destroy her, but they'd all have their turn and by the time she reached her second decade on earth

she would have been abused in almost every way but still, she wouldn't learn.

She didn't stand a chance; there were predators and temptations everywhere she glanced, each more charming and convincing than the last.

Finally, she'd live a life of slow, painful self-destruction, hating herself for making the same mistakes as the past.

This is what the devil wanted.

He summoned evil earth predators to be her father, uncles and grandfathers.

He also summoned men and women both young and old to pose as boyfriends and friends.

He lingered in them and temporarily possessed them so as to torture her in the end.

He even put insensitive professionals in her path

To try to drive her crazy,

As she cried and screamed they laughed.

However, although cursed by the Devil, the girl had God's protection and the protection of the angels.

Although the Devil cursed her with a heartless cowardly father, God blessed her with a woman with the biggest heart- a protective mother.

He chose for her a woman full of good. God gave her the best mother for her;

A mother who would never give up on her, who would fight the devil himself for the future of her child, and who would stand by her when no one else would.

A woman who possessed all the qualities the girl was bringing into the world and more;

A woman who believed the life of a child was worth fighting for.

To help the girl God not only blessed her with an extraordinary mother,
He also chose for her the perfect brother.
This way, although all other male family members were evil or sick and although all boyfriends were abusive, she'd always know how a good man would be
And that although there are some bad ones, there are also some good ones, to the contrary.
To help her along the way,
He also chose for her many angels, above and on earth, to be in the right place.

So, the girl was corrupted by her father and violated by almost all men she trusted after and she became a woman.
Somehow though, she didn't stop trusting others when she should, she stopped trusting herself when she shouldn't.
Then, the Devil saw how he could turn her good qualities into bad. She was an optimistic idealist, so forgiving and naïve, perhaps she would stand by an evil man or could be persuaded to lie,
And he became determined, not to merely destroy her, but to bring her to the dark side.

But God had major plans for the woman, like he does for all his children,
She had potential and was full of Good.
He refused to give up on her, and don't forget she had a mother who never would.

God and angels and her mother and brother had all been fighting to save her soul but still she seemed to be drifting to the dark side.

Now self-sabotaging because she was ashamed, it was herself she blamed, and she felt she had too much to hide and now she'd lost her sense of pride.

It was just too easy to do bad and too hard to good now.

She wanted to change and live the life God planned for her but she didn't know how.

Then she realized, she was the only one who could fight the battle with the devil and save her soul.

It was useless if she was working with the bad to destroy herself and self-sabotaging was taking its toll.

She needed to protect herself, cherish herself and forgive herself.

She needed to fight this battle now; it wasn't up to anyone else.

So, she fought the devil and all of his obstacles

And she fought and she fought and she fought

One battle at a time no matter whom or what presented as a threat and she realized she wasn't as helpless as she'd thought.

God's power, the power of angels, as well as the unconditional love of her mother and brother and finally her own free will;

The power of choice and her choice to fight to live a good life all combined, were the ingredients it took to break the devil's spell.

She shared the cure with everyone she could find who was still suffering.

Now, instead of more bad there is good, instead of more tears there is laughter,
And that's how
She lived
Happily ever after.

Chapter 1
Anger as Fuel

Refuse Retaliation

Creator, Higher Power of all that is good,
Help me.
Don't let them ruin me. Set me free.
Give me the strength to walk away from those who are toxic.
Help me apply my wisdom and logic.
When I'm about to lower myself to their level I must stop it.

I must not retaliate.
However, this would be easier to do if others would listen and validate.
But I won't let my anger turn to hate, I will use it as fuel to expose those so cruel
And create literature
For those to relate to who still suffer.

What Doesn't Kill You Makes You Stronger

After being tricked
I get smarter.
After each kick
I fight harder.
After being used
I appreciate myself more.
After being abused
I'm more cautious and less blinded than before.
After being robbed of all that I had
I cherish the priceless gifts I'm left with.
After I've sobbed, left alone, confused and sad,
I realize all I need is *myself* and I accept this.
After being humiliated
I still hold my head high.
After being violated
I don't blame myself and I no longer wonder why.
After being misjudged
I prove them wrong.
After having every reason to hold a grudge, I let go and move on.
After being misled, I work harder to find my way.
After they played games with my head, I learned to listen to what my inner voice has to say.
Each bad experience has taught be valuable lessons.
Each attack has made me stronger.
If I apply what I've learned
I won't be a victim any longer.
I will proudly be a survivor.

Don't Look Behind, Don't Look Ahead

I've been used, violated, abused and jaded.
I've been mistreated and hated.
I've been robbed over and over again, by strangers and friends,
Left shocked every time, and betrayed in the end.

But what in life have I lost, and what have I learned?
I've lost countless, desirable, materialistic items but what have I earned?
Self-respect, lessons, knowledge of predator's tactics to expect,
And so, I no longer yearn.
I don't look back, that way I don't trip.
I don't look too far ahead,
That way there's nothing I miss.

Chapter 2
Resilience

Gentle Power

The gentle power, like a delicate flower has to stop you in your tracks and make you do a double take
To look a little closer and investigate what it is about its understated state
That makes it possess such a unique, indescribable trait.
The gentle power like that of silence…
That is able to help you find your center, see clearer
And feel better able to entrance and expand consciousness.

The power I speak of isn't dominating, overbearing or dictating.
It isn't bold; it isn't bragged about or spoken about. It has gone untold.
Unlike powerful muscles, it strengthens rather than weakens as we grow old.

It's like the gentle power of a sunset that brings peace and allows us to forget our regrets.
Like the soft, silent wind that blows off your hat,
The strong sense of serenity you get from sitting at a still lake
Or the innocent power of an infant to entirely consume your every waking day.
That's the way my gentle power resonates.
The gentle power we women possess and our foremothers quietly create.

Path of the Empath

Do not hesitate child, you know what to do.
Continue to progress forward, you have the strength in you.
It is in your heart, it is in your soul,
It can be seen in your eyes and heard in the words you speak
It is yours; it is you – beautifully whole.
You have used this inner strength to survive,
Now own it, master it, and use it to thrive.

"But I am only me; this power is so great,
What if I can't master it before it's too late?
There is so much to do, but I don't know where to start,
And the memories of the past and realities of today weigh heavily on my heart."

Do not fear my child. Yes; you are only you.
You're the only one who can master the innate power bestowed on to you,
So who else could undertake this feat more genuinely and true?
Only you my child, only you.

And although it's overwhelming and you don't know where to start,
Start anywhere. Start with anything as long as it's positive and comes from the heart.

I know your heart is sore. You have been through so much.
The fact you feel your pain and the pain of the world shows you've never hardened and you've never lost touch.

Your heart is so good and pure; your mind is brilliant.
Words so wise, powerful eyes,
You my dear are resilient.

Elements of Me

I am the sky …
My bad moods are very dark and my good moods are very bright
Just as the sky changes from day to night.
I'm there for others though few others are there for me
As the sky holds the sun, the moon, the stars, the clouds
But what holds the sky?

I am the ocean …
I am deep and no one knows the potential I have within me,
As no one knows what treasures are still hidden deep within the ocean that are yet to be seen.

I am the wind; powerful, yet unseen.
I am the lake; sitting calm and serene.
There are traces within me of the elements which surround me
If you ask me what my power sources are, I'll tell you it is these.

Never Give Up

You have been blessed.
What's next?
Expect another test.
Do your best.
Learn from past regrets.
Don't forget. Don't fret.
Peace will come yet
As surely as the sun will set.
All you need is the inner strength you kept
Even as you wept.
As long as you hold onto that
It's not over yet.

"I've been *pushed and pushed and pushed*
And *shushed and shushed and shushed,*
But I will not be silenced.
I fight with heart, not with violence."

Chapter 3
The Fighter

Gradual Evolution

As I've grown throughout the years there's much I've learned.
I've shed many tears and struggled for what I've earned.
Still, I yearn.
The determination of my mother has taught me not to accept defeat.
The example set by my father drastically influenced how I allowed men to treat me.
I continue to learn.

I've been here so many times before, yet there's still so much to see.
What is the Creator trying to teach me?
Angels, guide me slowly.

I'm willing to do what I've always been meant to
And finally I will rest in peace for eternity when my mission is complete.
This is my last life here
And in my second decade, I finally live free of fear.

My life purpose – my *true life purpose*
Means more than anything to me.
It means much more than popularity or money.
I must prepare to accomplish it with clarity.

Unbreakable Warrioress

I cannot be defeated.
I am in this world because I am needed.
Without money and without intimidation I have power
Because I've held onto my strength no matter how beat down and no matter how hurt.
I have a mother who has taught me how strong I can be
And I have a brother who has showed me what a good man should be.

People don't realize that strength lies in the one who has had many past lives.
The strongest are those who overcome traumatic experiences, those who believe in synchronicity, not coincidences.
She is underestimated.
They don't understand the power she holds.
The power she was born with is the type of power that has been silenced and goes untold.

Better Me Enemy

I've got revenge on my mind but I pretend I'm fine.
My eyes are full of fears,
And no one realized,
I'm holding back the urge to cry,
But I'm on the verge of tears.

As a child I was exploited and violated
After a while as an adult, I became jaded.
I keep going, although not knowing how I'll cope.
I keep going, showing signs of hope.

Rob me and strip me of everything but my soul
And I'll still be better than you as a whole.
There are certain things you can't take and there are some things you can never control.

Cause me more anger because I'll just get stronger.
Try to kill me; I'll live longer.
Strip me of my identity and I'll make a new name for myself and become a better entity.
Try to drive me crazy and make me question my perception of reality
I'll re-evaluate and investigate and see even more clearly.

You can misuse me and abuse me,
Call me names or falsely accuse me
Because humiliation brings anger and anger produces determination.

Thank you.
You're making a very powerful, determined person.

Cause me more pain, try to place blame
Because I'll reach fame and expose your game.
You can read about me someday
And hear what the critics have to say.

When I expose the truth in my books,
When you see me walk by and everyone looks,
When I discover who I am, when I take a stand,
When I transform you won't even recognize me and you'll be no more than a vague memory.
When you see me walk by you'll look the other way,
FINALLY,
You'll have nothing to say.
You'll no longer be a threat
Because I am no longer prey.

Fight Like a Girl

I fight like a girl because it's just me against the world.
I've been beat by a guy twice my size and walked away.
I've stared the devil's advocate in the eyes, was once tricked by his lies, but proudly stand free from him today.

So, fight like a girl who has been underestimated her entire life.
Fight twice as hard, with twice your might.
They see us as prey, they see us as weak
So, fight like a girl- impossible to defeat.
Fight fiercely, fearlessly.
I've always been on guard and have spent my life trying to survive against the beasts.

I fight like a girl fighting for what is mine:
My family, my dignity, my life, my pride.
I fight because I refuse to hide.
I've been *pushed and pushed and pushed*
And *shushed and shushed and shushed,*
But I will not be silenced.
I fight with heart, not with violence.

I fight like a girl who has always had to fight.
I fight with my life on the line.
I fight for what's right, never stupidity, jealousy or spite.
With nothing left, I have nothing to lose.
Fighting's all I ever knew.
I'll fight for freedom, fairness, I'll fight for what's right.
Fight like a girl, fighting for your life.

Actually, I Can

Help me stay calm, help me stay sane.
In a world that disgusts me, help me promote change.
It may seem a poor woman can't win when up against a rich man
But actually, *I can.*

Even when I feel discouraged and think I can't keep going,
When weakness is showing and strength is slowing,
When it appears I cannot defeat the evil enemy's hand,
Actually, *I can.*

She's a word warrior
And if you think set-backs and barriers will destroy her,
If you think I'm vulnerable or unable,
You underestimate me but perhaps soon you will understand
Although my mind, body and spirit were attacked, and they think I can't fight back,
Actually, *I can.*

Chapter 4
Prayers

Bless

Bless thy people.
Help all those who are struggling, ease their pain.
If you're about to slip, may you refrain.
And help the privileged.
Bless them with awareness and empathy
Whenever they can help the less fortunate, may they display
a loving heart and generosity.

Bless thy animals.
They can be teachers and healers.
They have intelligence, awareness and each species is unique.
Let us protect them, defend them and respect them before it's too late and any more are extinct.

Bless thy Mother Earth who provides us land, water and food. Nourishment, security and opportunities are available through you.
We all walk on the ground of the same earth; May we do so with gratitude.

Bless thy birds, beautiful winged creatures that fly.
Bless thy sun, bless thy stars, bless thy moon in Father Sky.
Bless thy plants and thy trees that provide us oxygen, shelter, fruits, and many more life sustaining things.
Bless the North, bless the South, bless the West, bless the East,
Bless the earth, bless the water, bless the air, bless the fire,
Bless those I despise, bless those I admire.
Bless all people, bless all things.

Spirit Guide, Help Me

I call upon my Spirit Guide in times of duress.
I call upon you to lead me toward my true purpose.
And as I walk the path I was meant to take,
Help me to help others along the way.

Help me be a voice for those still silent.
Help me inspire peace in a world so violent.
Help me share the light with those still struggling in the dark.
Help me to always keep an open mind and a humble heart.

In times of Stress

Slow me down.
Allow me to cherish what I've found.
Ease my pain and help me refrain
From anything that is not good.
It may feel like I can't keep going but I know I should.

I will seek harsh truth before false flattery.
I'll seek love not lust and overlook ideals to accept reality.
And even if it's challenging, I'll walk away from the tempting if my intuition tells me I should.
It is angels that guide me and I have faith they are always beside me.
It is inherent woman wisdom my mother gave me, you see.
Angels, allow me to complete my purpose.
If I learn lessons and share the blessings, it will all be worth it.

Angelic Alignment

Angels of the morning,
Help me fight
The demons of the night.

While I work toward healing myself
I call on Archangel Raphael.
Invoking angels I light white candles and burn sage while I sit at my angel alter,
Spiritually aware, striving to understand
The transmuting rays of the fourth dimension,
Not allowing my faith to falter.

I need to know what the sign meant,
I know I have an imperative spiritual assignment,
So I practice angelic alignment.

I quiet my mind,
And I cleanse my aura,
I balance my chakras,
And I search within to find
The messages my angels sent to me when I was spiritually numb and blind.

I study the three triads, the three pillars, the three parts of the soul
And I strive to utilize maximum potential.
I am a Light Worker and I work hard,

Protected by my personal guardian angel that is always on guard.

I'm starving my demons – making sure my angels are well fed.

I am angelically led.

Through personal contact with my guardian angel, I will get ahead.

I study angels of the Kabala, Christian angels, Hindu angels, angels of the Buddha, Celtic angels, the Phoenix and the Thunderbird.

I call on all thy angels as I write thy sacred written word.

Spirit Guide by my Side

I surrender myself to you completely,
Today and for the rest of my life I trust in your plan for me.
I pray to you to please guide me and help me to stay on the Noble Path.
I want to live the life I was intended to lead at last.

Help me to apply forgiveness.
Allow me to receive this and allow me to give this.
Please provide me relief from negative thoughts and feelings.
Forgive me for my past mistakes,
Release all bitterness and hate.

Please give me the strength to react to cruelty and hatred with a loving heart and peaceful mind.
Although I wish to see no evil I do not wish to go blind.
So just help me to still see the good. The good is all around me waiting for me to find.
Help me face whatever challenges come my way and help me stay focused throughout all I do.
I feel you within and all around me, providing whatever I need and guiding me,
Thank you.

"There are many things that aren't in our control,
and many things that are in our control.
As they say, is the glass half empty
or is the glass half full?"

Chapter 5
Gratitude

Dear Mom

I wouldn't have been born without you and I couldn't have survived this life without you.
When I was born in the hospital, it was just us two.
Our connection was formed and it grew and grew and grew. You provided for me physically, emotionally, spiritually, financially. You were always there.
You always reminded me of my worth and you taught me what unconditional love is. No other love can compare.
When I was a little girl and you tucked me in at night, you'd say, "Who loves you?"
I played around then, but to tell you the truth, I knew then and I know now that at the top of the list has always been you.
There is no other woman I've known as dedicated, modest, selfless, empathetic, hard-working and true.
I wish I followed in the footsteps of my mother and brother,
But on some level, although I knew I had your love I sought it from another
And when I didn't get it from where I needed it I turned to others.
They do say a girl needs her father.
Yet, you were enough all along and you and my brother are all I need today
Because where I've been and what I've seen, I'm beyond blessed to have even one parent or person who never strayed.
Even when the cops said, "Don't worry, she'll be alright",
You were out searching the streets for your child all night -many, many nights.

When I found myself across the province, arrested and placed in a group home,
It was you who visited and it was you who answered the phone.
When people said, "If I were you I'd just kick her out",
You never went that route, I was never alone because I always had you and that is part of what saved me, without a doubt.
I am so sorry that after you tried so hard to make a good family name,
I made so many bad choices, for which I am so ashamed.
I wish I could go back, but then today our bond wouldn't quite be the same.
Thank you for surprises from "Ignore" and for washing my "grumpies" down the drain.
Thank you for showing up when I was hospitalized for depression at fourteen and no one else came.
(In order to prevent getting sued I will not name a name).
Now that I am a woman I see things in a different way
And although I always had immense respect for you, I have a whole new level of respect for you today.
Our bond is stronger now than ever and things are only going to get better.
Throughout the darkness and during the light,
We're still moving along...
Side by side.

My Brother, My Hero

I wish I followed your guidance and stuck with you.
I could have been so different; life could have been so different
But it isn't and I didn't. I was lost and confused.
You are someone who has always had my best interests in your heart and your mind.
You are someone who never turned your back on me. There's not many of these people and they're hard to find.
I wish I could go back. I'd tell *myself* don't be stupid and give myself a slap.
I never should have strayed, I wish I would have followed your leadership and stayed on the right path but I'll do whatever I can to make sure at last, we're closer than ever today.
We are basically the only family we have.
I value your support; I respect how you are true to yourself. Throughout all the darkness, you know, it was you and mom and no one else.
There may not be enough of us to form a family circle,
But we made it through the darkness. We are one damn strong triangle.
Playing in the swamp, bringing Lilly home to mom, ferrets, and "green face",
These are real memories we have that cannot be erased.
Then there were the dark times, your own sister acting like a disgrace, introducing boyfriend's twice our age, and although I can't remember, I can't forget your most significant graduation day,

I'm so, so sorry. I'm sorry I've messed up in so many ways. I'm sorry I've made so many mistakes. I want to be close as brother and sister and as friends, and I'll do whatever it takes.

Thank you for always being there and for never walking away.

They say you shouldn't idolize a human being but I view you and mom almost as saints. That's what you've been for me. You have always been a leader; you have always been true to yourself.

You never conform and you never try to impress anyone else. You have skills and talents I admire, you have more self-discipline, modesty and humility than anyone I know.

It's impossible for me not to idolize you. You are my hero.

Sources of Hope

Everything is wrong, everything's a mess.
Crying and alone, out of the corner of my eye through the window, I notice the sunset.
Intertwined in the sky are colors of pink, orange and blue.
I see layers and layers of depths of colors, fluorescent in their hue.
The sky is so beautiful and the world is so dreadful; it seems surreal.
I reach out of my window to touch it but it's not something I can feel.
Are people deserving of this beautiful world and this vast colorful sky?
People are preoccupied and rush through life, rarely stopping to watch the sunset as they go by.

I am consumed by negative energy
And it's assumed I've been defeated by my enemy.
I despise this life of lies,
But it was because I cried, alone in my room,
That I saw the sunset that night.
The sunset became my source of hope to cope.
Everything happens for a reason and the rising of the sacred sun provided something I could believe in.

Counting Blessings

Give gratitude and maintain a positive attitude.
There is always so much to be grateful for.
Once I've counted my blessings, I always find more.

Thank you for my family who always stood by me.
We are a strong family unit, even if only of three.
Thank you for this moment. I am content, I am safe, and I am free.
Thank you for my gifts and abilities,
All the talents and capabilities I've been blessed with individually and as a human being.
I have shelter, I have food,
There are so many reasons to say "Thank you".

And let us not forget the little things,
The flowers and the birds that sing.
Puddles for splashing and footballs for catching,
Picnics and flying kites,
Star gazing, serene sights, and cool summer nights.
Snow angels and climbing trees,
The calm lake and the cool breeze.

Give gratitude
For the many blessings granted to you.
Count your blessings each day.
Let go of what you've lost; focus on what you've gained.
If you think the glass is half empty, reframe.
If you think you can't keep going,
Remember how far you already came.

Find the Good

When you feel like you can't cope,
When you're losing hope,
When you want to hang your head in despair thinking life's not fair,
Look up instead, and find the good,
It's everywhere.

An elderly couple holding hands,
A father with his kids making castles in the sand,
A kitten sleeping peacefully,
Little girls skipping gleefully
The sunshine after the rain
And the beautiful rainbow that came.
After the storm passed; Beauty and peace at last.
The smell of a camp fire,
Gardens to admire.
A forest of pine trees covered in snow,
A cherished memory from long ago,
Oceans, mountains, trees, a beach, flowers, a field,
If ever doubting your connection to the universe, look around to know it's real.

"She's a solo soul, shattered, yet whole;
She's a word warrioress with a sacred purpose."

Chapter 6
The Survivor

Watch What I Can Do

There's not much left to write, not much point to fight unless out of spite which I'm told isn't right, despite the sight of him thinking he's won when he goes to sleep tonight.
I lost blood, I lost love, I lost my baby and I thought maybe I'd hit rock bottom there.
But then, I lost my sanity, I lost my job, I felt numb, I felt robbed, and nobody cared.
She sits still, staring at the paper with a pen in her hand thinking of what to write before she falls asleep tonight.
She hopes to understand what step to take, what source of hope will force her to cope and live her life a new way.
She contemplates what it will take for her to feel as though she's succeeded
And live her life with purpose in the way she was needed.
She stands undefeated,
Yet she cries silently from deep within her soul,
Desperate cries to society to see the picture as a whole.
She lives with oppression, like many in her situation
So she'll argue it and defy it.
She has never been one to keep quiet.
She's done sitting still.
They think she can't move forward but she will.
She has always lived with barriers
But they no longer stop her because she's been through worse and she's been through scarier.
So either get out of the way or let me through
And watch what I can do.

The Never Ending Battle

In this never ending battle, you've been the only one to fight.
Provoked, choked, belittled by the words you spoke,
I never fought back and always tried to keep the peace.
After fighting for so long it's inevitable, you're going to get weak.
And after what you did to me, when Karma intervenes, your future is bleak.
You cannot defeat me. I'm not engaged in the fighting.
While you were fighting; before, during and after,
I became stronger, smarter and faster.
I learn so much from my adversaries, soon each skill I will master.

Perfectly Broken & Forever Whole

You are alive.
You are capable and strong.
You wish for peace and happiness; for this we all long.
You are a human. You are a woman. You are an individual.
You are perfectly broken and forever whole.

Untitled

I'm an angel with no halo,
I'm innocent if you say so.
I'm a wolf's fang,
I defeated the rivalry gang.
I'm not what I seem,
I'm nothing you've seen.
I'm a role model, I'm a disgrace.
I'm shy but I'm looking you square in the face.
I'm the flame of a blazing fire,
I'm the squeal of a muscle car's tire.
I've seen enough and been quiet for as long as I possibly could have been.
Now I'd like to debate you and although I'd hate to cause a scene
I need to wake you; Come back to reality, it's all a dream.
The world's not as you sit on your high horse and claim it to be.

Untitled

Her face stares into space, thinking about all the memories she wishes she could erase.
Why did he have to change? Things will never be the same.
All of her love went to waste because he would never appreciate or love her in a healthy way.

But she's strong and he was wrong.
He's gone and she's moved on.
Her head's still held high and someday he might wonder why he never even tried,
And how he could act careless as she cried,
But even if he doesn't she will survive.

I'm Strong when you're Gone

As I stay strong, as I hold my head high,
In order To capture my heart back from your grip, I must pry.
Just like an addiction, I must take it one day at a time.
I must heal my heart with my own power,
But when you say you care I cower.
I don't want to believe your lies. I don't want to spin in the same cycle we've known.
When I break free from you, I see the truth and without you I've grown.
I know what I want and though it seems out of reach,
I know it's only so distant in order to teach
That sacrifice and struggle can be good
Because you may appreciate things that you never before could.
I may only be a girl in the eyes of a man,
But I stand alone and need no clan.
I'm still strong when you're gone
Because even when each petal of the rose has drifted away,
The root of the flower still remains.

Solo Soul

Which battle do I fight?
Which letter do I write?
Where do I begin?
How do I not react when people act out of spite?
How do I relax and sit back and keep telling myself it's alright
When it's ALL wrong and it seems I can't win?

When I put my trust in people, I'm reminded again and again why I shouldn't.
Yet, I keep giving chances and letting people in although I promised myself last time I wouldn't.
I told myself I'd stop trusting, stop caring, stop having faith and hope, but I couldn't.

I refuse to believe that everyone is the same as those I've seen.
I refuse to believe that everyone deceives and the people in the world I live in are all consumed by greed.
Although it seems we value one's self-worth by their net worth,
Although it could be perceived I'm naïve,
Contrary to what they would have me believe
I was as valuable as a royal princess since birth
To the woman and the Higher Power who created me.
They have never let me down, so no matter what anyone says or does it is them I believe
And they tell me that I am a precious, highly capable being.

Even if I have nothing; no money or valuable things, at least I didn't lie, steal or cheat.
Even if part of why I have nothing is because people robbed, conned or used me,
At least I saw their true colors
And even if find myself alone, at least it's because I've grown so this is what I've chosen;
To be used and abused by no others.

Indigo Child

Despite what they've told you, despite what your diagnosis may say,
You are okay.
Even when you hit a writer's block, when you try to speak but can't talk, when the thoughts won't stop,
You are okay.

Defiance
Is more rational than compliance
When asked to comply with tyrants.
May the truth seekers, light seers, dream believers all form an alliance!

We will never conform,
We will never follow the norm.
We deserve more!

It is normal and expected to feel discontented
When our people are becoming more disconnected
Our planet and our species are in crisis:
There's poverty, global warming, animal extinction, wars and ISIS.
It is natural to feel anxiety
When you can't trust your government or the police.
There's so much corruption and brutality.
All we see is more corruption and all we see is the corrupt win,
From police, to priests, to politicians.
So we make no apology for our interruption, we just walk in.
Speak up Indigo children, *you are the chosen.*

Unbreakable

I've made many mistakes but they've showed me what it takes to create a positive fate.
I've literally died and without being revived somehow survived and came back to life.
I've quit a serious cocaine habit overnight
And beat a crack addiction after a more difficult fight.
For a long time I've answered to a different name.
I've been outside of my domain, numb from pain.
I had no fixed address,
In my suitcase was all I had left.
I lived out of that bag in bar houses and feared the sun rising.
I'd walk all night analyzing options I had.
I planned on revising my life and making things right by somehow getting on track.
I won't concentrate on the hate that seems to be every man's dominant trait.
I'll appreciate myself for my mother's sake.
I won't wait until it's too late, I won't back down and I won't fake what I have to say.
I'll make, break, give, take, honor and appreciate
And although my heart may ache,
Each day, I'll wake.

Her Choice

The one who does her own thing, her own way is the one who leaves her mark;
The one who follows her feelings and trusts her heart.
Mysterious and intriguing, she follows her feelings.
She started with almost no one and nothing.
She cut ties, earned trust, confessed lies and now she lives in faith and practices acceptance.
She shows gratitude and stepped up to her last chance.
Now she expects no less than the best and accepts no disrespect.
She's vowed to protect whatever she has left.
She has no time to waste
And can't afford to make even one more of the same mistakes.
She is a young woman on a mission,
Past regrets are her ammunition.
Past perpetrators provide her fuel
And innate survival mechanisms are her tools.
She continuously tries to better herself
And doesn't allow herself to get attached to anyone or anything else.
Buddhist principals
And words whimsical,
Abnormal and atypical,
Almost all are critical
But she's found her voice.
She's made her choice
Between revenge and rejoice.

Guarded

They disrespect me because they expect me to accept thee, to react quietly, passively
But they have me confused with the old me and I'm smarter and stronger than I've ever been.
The obscene, the mean, the drama queen, the dad who's never been,
I protect myself from them, don't subject myself to them
Because there's too much they've already ruined.
I know I can't trust them, it's already been proven.

So run your mouth, try to create doubt, judge me, while never considering what you're all about.
I'll write you off and you'll cease to exist. The beauty of it is this: I don't have to deal with your shit if I don't subject myself to it.

Everyone wants a piece of me- just that *one* piece of me.
I'll get my satisfaction by not giving them a reaction.
They either love me or hate me, friends or enemies, no in between.
But they're not friends or enemies of mine,
They no longer impact my daily life.
I have big plans and every moment is precious.
They disrespect me but I expect it,
Now I remove myself so as to ensure my mind, body and soul are protected.

The Day I Came Back to Life

Today, the "old me" died.
I screamed, I grieved and I cried.
The one who my enemies created,
The one who was weak and jaded,
I was desperate for love and protection,
I wasn't careful enough who I let in
And I made mistake after mistake.
I'd give and give and give and they'd take, take, take.
I lost touch with who my mom made, who my God made,
And I became fake.

The one who doubted myself and trusted everyone else.
The one who became my own worst enemy,
The girl you violated, they used, he humiliated and he abused,
She is dead.
The girl who was easy prey,
That girl who was messed up and full of hate, she died today
And there's nothing left of her for you to take.
You killed her.
A new woman was born, my newfound self was formed and there's nothing about her that's familiar.

I will not trust others until they prove themselves
And I won't feel selfish if I don't put anyone above myself.
I won't tolerate mistreatment or disrespect.
I will stand my ground.
These are my vows:

I vow to love and cherish myself,
I vow to value family over wealth.
I vow to avoid negative people, places and things,
I vow to reflect on what each of my life lessons mean.
These are my vows, and I am the newfound, improved version of me.

Chapter 7
Wisdom

Words to Live By

Give it everything.
Expect nothing.

Love your enemies.
Love them for what they taught you.
Count your blessings
And know God hasn't forgot you.
Love your enemies from afar.
You can do this because God is within.

Nurture your good qualities and work to minimize the bad. Strive for balance and begin by working with what you already have.

Learn to hold on to what deserves to be cherished
And let go of the negative and allow it to perish.

Let go of ideals and let everything happen to you.
You don't need anyone to give you the answers. Inside of you, you know what's true.

Do not live for praise,
You don't need it.
Learn from the past and refuse to repeat it.
When you put your trust in the universe, it no longer hurts when you hear man's cruel words.
As you learn from the past; dream for the future but live in the now.
Persistently ponder and practice how.

Acknowledge, accept and let go of past pain.
Think of the resilient rainbow consequently resulting from the rain.
Awaken your soul
By quieting your mind,
You already possess
What you're trying to find.

Maintain a compassionate, giving nature
While simultaneously protecting yourself from master manipulators.

Learn to read and read to learn.
Learn so you can teach, teach so you can inspire and reach,
Accept yourself even when weak
Because when you overcome your weakest moments your inner strength is at its peak.

If I Knew Then What I Know Now

If I knew then what I know now,
I would have followed the guidance of my mother and brother.
When it comes to others, I never would have bothered.
When I said other family members were dead to me in grade two, that's the story I would have stuck to.
It would have spared me so much of the pain I went through.

If I knew then what I know now, I wouldn't have doubted my abilities,
I would have excelled in school and been on every team.
I'd stick up for myself and I wouldn't let others push me around
If I knew then what I know now.

I wouldn't have let others influence *my* choice,
I wouldn't let them use my body; I'd make them listen to my voice.
I would have acted my age.
I would have allowed myself to go through each developmental stage.
If I knew then what I know now, as a child I wouldn't have kept secrets for adults
And I wouldn't have believed that what they did to me was my fault.

I would have seen through him and him and him, and I wouldn't have wanted anything to do with them.

I would have cried in my mom's arms instead of pushing her away.
I would have followed her example and I never would have strayed.

While I still could, I would have cherished being a little girl.
I would have owned that purity and not desperately tried to conform and follow the norm and the rules in a man's world.
I wouldn't have wished to be a boy, I would have been proud to be a girl.
As a child, I wouldn't have dressed and acted like a boy and pretended I was what I was not.
I missed out on being me; my likes, my interests, my thoughts.
Then as a teen, I wouldn't have dressed like a woman, I would have accepted I was still a girl.
I would have loved myself as I was, instead of looking for love somewhere else, and getting lost in the world.
It seemed my sexuality was all they'd see, but if I knew then what I know now, I wouldn't have let it define me.
(And I would have worn heels less and saved my feet).

If I knew then what I know now, I wouldn't have gone with that guy or told that lie,
I wouldn't have smoked that first smoke or toke, drank that first drink, ate that first pill, or did that first line.
I would never have said yes to please others, each choice would be made with *my* best interests in mind.
If I knew then what I know now, I would have recognized: There is kind and then there is blind.
Oh, how I wish I could press rewind.
Oh, how I wish I had left at the first warning sign.

I would never have let them use me.
I'd know my worth and I would never let them confuse me.
I wouldn't have cared about fitting in because there was no chance of truly fitting in until I knew myself.
I lost so much valuable time by trying to please everyone else.
I would have cherished my body, spirit and mind.
I would have followed my intuition and made sure my thoughts and behavior were aligned.

I would have spoken up more and allowed them to talk down to me less.
I would have challenged myself and given it my best.
I would have considered how my actions would impact the couple of people who actually cared.
I never would have caused them pain, panic, shame, needless fights, sleepless nights and despair.
I look back at everything I've been through. My life has forever changed; things got so bad and I wonder how.
I know things could have been so different had I known then what I know now.

Lessons Learned

Our choices
Will impact our life.
Our voices
Can win the fight.

As powerful as loud and proud is silent and humble.
What do we all require in the dark?
A light or a guide so we don't stumble.

It is imperative that we always protect ourselves
Because you are a precious gift inside a soft shell.
Worrying about where you may be in the future or regretting what you did in the past is a waste of time
Because you end up missing the present moment and in that moment you could discover what you're here to find.

Spend time with animals, be cautious of man, and always respect thy land.
Day dream and soul search, go to your inner church, diligently do self-work. Study, practice and question until you understand.
And if you see someone trying to find the light and are in a position where you can, always lend a helping hand.

Feeding the Soul

Keep your heart free from hate
Keep your mind free from worry.
Live simply.
Dream big.
Expect nothing.
Give it everything.
Fill your life with love.
Scatter inspiration and light.
Feed the birds.
Don't believe everything you've heard.
Always be true to your word.
Protect self.
Help others.

The Warrior's Stance

I walk toward the moon, against the gloom.
I was nurtured in the wise woman's womb.
I'm working toward reaching self-actualization soon.
I stand still in the warrior's stance.
And I pounce on opportunity and chance.

Treat Yourself How you Wish to be Treated

All the giving of understanding, compassion, and encouragement that I have given to others,
Had I given the same to myself, I would be free of guilt and shame and self-doubt.
All of the red flags and warning signs I've seen,
Had I taken them seriously and paid attention to each
I may not have had even one major catastrophe.
All of the comfort and kind words and forgiveness that I have given to others,
Had I have given the same to myself I would feel safe and hopeful and free.
All of the time, energy and effort that I have given to others, had I have given the same amount to myself, who knows where I would be.
Do onto others how you would have them do onto you; that is the Golden Rule.
But don't forget to treat yourself as well as you treat others, alas be made a fool.

Natural Resources

I get my energy
From the rising of the sacred sun and the feeling of the soft morning breeze.
I get my oxygen from the trees.

I find inspiration in the mystical rainbow after the rain
And a loving animal always soothes my pain.

I find faith in the stars in the sky;
So vast, so mysterious, proof there's something beyond this.
It's only necessary to take it in, not to ask why.

Sitting silently in a forest, I gain insight.

On the beach in the sand I am rich.
Climbing a tree or making a snow angel enable everlasting youth of spirit
And a warm candle lit bubble bath is bliss.

Happiness is found in the sound of an infant's laughter.
It's contagious and can bring a smile to one's face long after.

I gain wisdom from nature.
A caterpillar transforming to a butterfly, century old trees and perennial flowers
Are just some of the magnificent, priceless wonders
And I don't have to go far.
They're all in my back yard.

Everything I need is either within me or all around me.
Greater than paper symbolizing money, it can't be bought or owned
It only exists
If left to be.

Be the Girl who Needs Nothing from No One

A man came into my life.
Our beliefs weren't quite aligned and although he was appealing in my eyes, deep down I knew he wasn't Mr. Right.
Still, he offered me everything I spent so long trying to seek,
Things I had always thought were important to me.
He was the most powerful man I ever met.
He was respected by many, feared by many and even worshiped by some.
He had many skills I admired and hoped to achieve.
He had all kinds of connections, and I had none.

He offered to protect me.
Although it's all I've ever wanted, I told him I don't need protection.
I'm in a different place now, in a different position.
I'm not afraid and I can and will protect myself.
That's my job. I just can't count on anyone else.

He told me he would love me
I told him that was sweet but I don't require the love of another; I'm learning to love myself.
For this, I don't need a man
And when I finally love myself I won't need to hold anyone's hand.

He said he'd mentor me and teach me things I desperately wanted to learn.
Although this seemed kind, still I couldn't fully trust him, because trust is earned.
I told him I don't need a mentor; Skills can be self-taught.
And even if a person offers me everything I want and need, I can't be bought.

He offered to use his connections to help me accomplish my dreams
But I know I live in a world where nothing is for free.
I thanked him but I don't need anything handed to me,
And ultimately,
I'm now comfortable struggling,
Because this way, when I accomplish my goals it's that much more rewarding.

Self-Reflection

Take time to self-reflect and ponder;
What do you see when you look at your reflection in the water?

You are on the Right Path

Look back and laugh,
Pamper yourself and relax.
You are on the right path.

"We ask ourselves, when will they catch up with us, when will they accept us like we accept them? And we fear for them when karma teaches them their lesson."

Chapter 8
Karma

The Man Who Seemingly Had it All & The Woman Who Seemingly Had Nothing

There was a man who seemingly had it all
His dream job, his dream bike, his dream car; He had assets and wealth.
He had luck on his side. He had his freedom and he had his health.
He had friends and family and always a good looking girlfriend to appeal to his vanity.
He was liked by many. He had a big, beautiful house and he slept in a comfortable, luxurious bed.
He never regretted anything he did or anything he said.
His life was full of exciting adventures and fun,
But the biggest gift of all was being blessed with a son.

However, although this man seemingly had it all, he was doomed because a long time ago he sold his soul.
And his over inflated sense of entitlement made him a selfish, narcissistic man.
Deep down he was spiritually discontent.
He had committed evil deeds and that brings me
To the woman who seemingly had nothing.

There was a woman who seemingly had nothing.
She had no partner, no children,
No house, no car, no assets, and little money to spend.
Although she was liked by many, she was targeted and misused by many as well.

And although she'd never sold her soul to the devil, she'd gone through hell.
Although she was half the man's age, she'd faced twice as many adversities and tragedies.
Yet, although it might seem like she had nothing going for her,
She'd triumph and succeed because she was a warrior
And because she had good intentions and a pure heart,
That was enough for God to grant her a fresh start.

The man who seemingly had everything could never have enough.
He was full of greed.
But she, the woman who seemingly had nothing, still counted every blessing.
She never gave up and always believed, until finally karma intervened.

No, the man did not lose everything.
He still possessed some very beautiful materialistic things.
Karma didn't take it all one by one,
However, the man did lose the most precious gift he had: the respect of his son.
And yes the woman seemingly had nothing but she still had the most important thing.
She had her life ahead of her and she'd only just begun.
Although the man had luck on his side,
The woman had God on hers, and although she wasn't yet where she wanted to be, she kept going and she tried and tried and tried.
When it comes to heart and soul and pride, now she has it all and he has none.

Evolution of the Spirit

Finally things are falling into place,
I've reclaimed my life and I'm not letting it go to waste.
After all the heartache, trauma and pain
No, I will never be the same.
I will be better.
When you see a woman determined to rise you better let her.
Those who damaged me and took advantage of me, those who turned their backs on me in my times of need now miss out on the beauty that is the transformation from lost, vulnerable girl to strong, wise woman.

Different Perceptions

They come at us at with ignorance and aggression.
We let them.
They are full of repressed rage, trapped in their own cage and trying to escape depression
But we are full of knowledge, wisdom and Zen.
We ask ourselves, when will they catch up with us, when will they accept us like we accept them?
And we fear for them when karma teaches them their lesson.
As we explore past life regression we learn that judgment depends on one's perception.

"What if we were all so in touch with
ourselves we were aware of our breathing?
What if we each stop doubting ourselves
and we all start believing?
What if we plant seeds, got rid of the weeds?
How beautiful our garden would be."

Chapter 9
Hope

Planetary Healing

Everything and everyone in the world is interconnected,
Yet now more than ever we're disconnected
Mistakes of the human race which led to global warming and extinction need to be corrected
Or very few souls will ever be resurrected.

Why do we care more about diamonds than the exploited children who mine them?
We don't care how it happens as long as someone finds them.
Why do we have hot dog eating contests where we eat until we're sick and buffets where we eat until it's uncomfortable to sit?
When there is a food shortage in other parts of the world and right in our own community there are hungry boys and girls? How do we justify it?
And at weddings, "the chicken's overcooked" and the fish is "too dry",
We push our plate aside after just a couple bites but this should be a crime considering all the hungry children who want seconds but are denied
Because there's not enough food in the food banks
And there are not enough community gardens,
So as you try to decide what to make for dinner make sure you give thanks, because you are blessed to have options.

Why are there so many children called "wards of the state"?
Too many children never know a stable family or a stable home and never get a break.
Why are there so many children who are neglected and abused?
And why are there so many adults continuing to create children they don't value?
Why is it that there are some people who have less maternal/paternal instinct than an animal?

In preparation for birth the polar bear goes up to eight months without eating,
So how is it that some women can't go nine without drinking?
Emperor penguins walk miles for their offspring,
An octopus will literally starve itself for its babies;
After laying her eggs she guards them ferociously.
She doesn't leave, not even to get food.
She's even been witnessed eating her own tentacles rather than leaving her brood.
After the eggs are hatched and drift away the mother often dies,
Either from famine or because she's too weak to defend herself from predators even if she tries;
She is a truly selfless mother and one of self-sacrifice.

And father wolves are attentive and protective
They hunt to provide food and take on a stern role as a mentor in the cub's life.
How is it that wolves co-parent better than many people as man and wife?

And how is that my own father had no instinct or desire to be my protector?
How is it that some people can harm their own child?
And we call the animals not the people wild?

Why do we continue cutting down trees when just one tree can provide us with so many things we need?
They help combat climate change, provide oxygen, save water, help conserve energy, and provide food to eat.
Medicinal plants can help fight disease; it's been said they're nature's pharmacy and I agree.
As we cut down the trees we put condos in their place.
Why do we stack people on top of each other and overpopulate our cities
While we decrease the amount of natural resources available to us provided by the trees?

Although the diamonds, the four course meals, having children, and building more condos for us to live in might seem appealing,
It is more urgent and imperative that we build on planetary healing.

Let us learn from the animals and protect and mentor our young.
Let's begin respecting and protecting our earth, let's start now as there is much to be done.
Let us honor thy land and respect thy sacred tree
And as we begin to connect with the earth, the animals and all sentient beings, let us never lose touch with this feeling
And we all may experience planetary healing.

What if?

What if no person took more than they need?
Perhaps then we'd all have enough.
What if we didn't operate on greed?
What if the privileged helped those who have it rough?

In a world of the haves and the have nots, what if the haves had not and the have nots had?
What if it were illegal for one person to possess a net worth of something absurd like a billion
And what if we shared the excess wealth with the hungry and sick children?
What if instead of using wheat, barley and yeast to produce alcohol, we used it to help combat world hunger?
I wonder.

What if we all made time to walk barefoot in the grass like ancestors of our past?
Transmuting electrons to our body, into ourselves,
By connecting our body to the earth we're inducing favorable electrophysiological alterations that promote optimal health.
What if we all cherished the Sacred Tree which the Creator has implanted for us all to meet and find healing and security?
What if we all valued the gifts of the four directions, like beautiful speech, respect for elders, generosity, and integrating all intellectual capacities?
I wonder how amazing the world would be.

What if we didn't worry today about tomorrow?
What if we were just grateful for today?
We worry about the future
But what if tomorrow never came?

What if each person followed their dreams
And we each used our gifts?
What if we all become better than what we've been?
What if, what if, what if?

If we use our potential,
If we nurture mind, body and soul,
If we all progress
Toward our Divine purpose,
If we settle for nothing less
Than the best and truly believe we are worth it,
If we love and do not hate,
If we do not destroy and we create,
If we raise our vibration rate,
If we are at peace and our minds don't race,
We don't take a break and it is proof of the mind's state,
But what if we all took the time to reflect, reduce stress and rejuvenate?
Or what if it were too late?

What if we all act now because tomorrow isn't guaranteed and all we have is today?
What if she was nice to her and he was nice to him, you were nice to me and we were nice to them?
What if there were no cliques and groups,

And no bullying on the playground, in the office, the House of Senate, in the media, on Facebook, Instagram and Youtube?
What if no one had anything to prove?

What if we were all genuine, free of insecurities and cared how others feel?
What if no one acted fake, what if we all acted real?
What if we respected mother earth and were kind to all beings?
What if we studied the ancient teachings?
What if we all practiced Right View, Right Thought, Right Speech, Right Conduct, Right Livelihood, Right Effort, Right Mindfulness, and Right Meditative Stabilization?
What if we all reach self-actualization?
What if we surrounded ourselves with positive stimulation?
What if we sat with ourselves and pondered until we came to a profound realization?
What if we were all so in touch with ourselves we were aware of our breathing?
What if we each stop doubting ourselves and we all start believing?
What if we plant seeds, got rid of the weeds? How beautiful our garden would be.

What if no one gave up but everyone wakes up?
What if we could hear the cries of all the desperate animals, all the struggling people, the land, the ocean, the sea and the trees?
Our entire planet would be overpowered by the united screams.

What if instead of top model, we aspired to be our positive role model?
What if we all had positive role models?
What if as a girl, rather than equate my worth to my sexuality, I was valued when I spoke intellectually?
If that got me even half as much attention, imagine how different things would be.
What if boys could cry and girls could scream?
Or what if we wake up and our whole life as we know it is a dream?

What if we emerge from a deep sleep, and suddenly we see everything clearly and we evolve spiritually?
What if we all have an awakening and reach a greater level of consciousness,
And as we experience this shift
Life on earth became full of beauty and bliss? What if?

Dear Dad

Dear Dad,

I did everything I could to get your attention but when I finally did it led to my regression.
When I think of my mom and how she's always been there I can't understand how you can have a daughter and not even act like you care.
It's been years since we've seen each other and talked and one of the last times I saw you, you told me to walk.
Well, I walked away and I am a very different person today.
Mistakes were made in my youth but now I'm an adult like you and I see things in a very different way.
Despite all the damage done, I still remember when I was really young and you read me a story.
I hope one day to hear your Kermit the Frog voice but that can't happen until I hear two words from you: "I'm sorry."
Anyone can be forgiven for their past but first they must ask Only then could we ever have a healthy relationship at last.

Chapter 10
Self Respect

Self-Help & Self Respect

If no one is helping you and everyone is letting you down,
Turn to thy self and use self-help to turn your life around.
Fight for your life, don't give up like they expect.
If no one is in your corner, all the more reason to conserve your strength;
It's a hard lesson to accept.
If no one is helping you, turn to self-help, and if they disrespect you practice self-respect.

Know your Role

You say I can be your bottom bitch but I say something's wrong with this.
He's hers, hers, hers, hers and I'm his?
I'm not your bottom bitch; I'm not your side chick,
I have pride which makes me the boss bitch.

The Book Doesn't Always Match the Cover

Some of the most respectful men I've known wore patches,
Some of those who terrorized me wore badges.
The book and the cover aren't always matches

Letting Go of the Old Alter Ego

When I was stripping and doing drugs it drained my soul.
Now that I'm finally living the life I was meant to, my dreams are coming true and I feel whole.
It's almost like getting back what the demons stole.
Give me a pen; Fuck the pole.

I'm That Girl

I'm that girl who doesn't want or need anything from anyone.
I'm that girl who will make it on her own.
I'm that girl who now sees through you, speaks the truth to you, and leaves if mutual respect isn't shown.
I'm that girl who has heard it all, so I no longer fall for their charm.
I'm that girl who doesn't need your attention or to be candy on your arm.
I'm not going to give it up just because of your social status or what's in your wallet and how fat it is.
I'm not going to give it up because of your name or your fame.
I don't care who you are, if you've broken my trust or tried to confuse love with lust, I'm going to call you on your game
Never again will I be compliant,
Again and again, I'll be defiant,
Even if up against a giant
Because *now* no one can control me
And *now* I demand equality.
I'm that girl who fought the devil and won
And I've only just begun.

A Personal Message from the Author

To those who are still struggling:
Be gentle with yourself and look within.
The question is not "can you change your life?" The question is "When will you begin?"
You have the power, the power of choice.
You have the gifts; the gifts of your visions, your dreams, your voice.
You are a survivor; *they can't break you.*
You are here, keep going and your life can be better than you ever knew.

To those who haven't struggled:
To those who haven't faced hardships like addiction and mental health issues or poverty or abuse,
To those who are insensitive to these issues and deny the truth,
Don't be quick to judge or quick to turn away those who have lost their way, because it could happen to you.
The stripper or sex worker they call a whore, maybe once upon a time she wanted more.
They lost all rights to judge her when they entered the strip club or opened the hotel room door.
Alcohol and strip clubs are basically socially acceptable; open your eyes.
And if there's someone you misjudged, apologize.
We may be completely different but we're still the same

If something isn't right, do whatever you can to create change.
It's your children who will inherit this earth, what kind of world do you want to leave them and what do you want them to gain?
And if the world's not right and you did nothing, who but yourself can you blame?

To my adversaries:
Thank you for giving me the motivation to prove you wrong.
I've accepted I don't need anyone, I'm only sorry it took me so long.
When you write someone off and your life suddenly gets better
This is an indication they weren't meant to be in it, so I don't send reconciliation letters.
To the evil and the sick, to the narcissists, I pray you will evolve and honor thy Great Spirit.
To those who violated my rights and to those who almost took my life
Back the fuck down because nothing will stop me. I have hope and faith and believe
Everything is going to be alright.

The darkness does exist, in many forms and many ways; you can hear it and feel it and see it.
It has become so normalized and glamorized through the government and the media's lies that we have become desensitized.
We lost touch with the ancient ways; we only honor what is man-made.

The people, the planet, the oceans and the seas, animals of all species are all suffering.

Yet, there is *still* light in sight.
There is survival and there is life.
Now more than ever we need to love and heal not hate and fight.
There is a metaphysical war, and it won't matter who is rich or poor,
Material possessions and physical surroundings will matter no more.
It is the battle of the darkness and the light.
It will not be a battle of armies; it will be a battle of the souls.
Are you doing harm, or are you doing what's right?
It is the battle of evil and good.
During the battle, it's not about if you did what you should, it's about if you did what you could.
Our planet will evolve or it will destruct.
We as people can make progress or we can regress.
The progress can't be all about technological success,
We are spiritual beings with a spiritual purpose.
The war is within and in order to win there must be *evolution of the spirit*.

Lightning Source UK Ltd.
Milton Keynes UK
UKOW01f0923240317
297246UK00004BA/19/P